CW00688505

SWANSEA'S
1939–45
FRONTLINE KIDS

JIM OWEN

AMBERLEY

First published 2014

Amberley Publishing
The Hill, Stroud, Gloucestershire, GL5 4EP
www.amberley-books.com

Copyright © Jim Owen, 2014

The right of Jim Owen to be identified as the Author
of this work has been asserted in accordance with the
Copyrights, Designs and Patents Act 1988.

ISBN 978 1 4456 4355 7 (print)
ISBN 978 1 4456 4391 5 (ebook)

All rights reserved. No part of this book may be
reprinted or reproduced or utilised in any form or by
any electronic, mechanical or other means, now known
or hereafter invented, including photocopying and
recording, or in any information storage or retrieval
system, without the permission in writing from the
Publishers.

British Library Cataloguing in Publication Data.
A catalogue record for this book is available from the
British Library.

Typesetting by Amberley Publishing.
Printed in Great Britain.

CONTENTS

PREFACE

With the Fall of France during the Second World War, Swansea came within striking range of the Luftwaffe. The town, an important industrial centre and strategically placed seaport, became a prime target. The German air force wasted little time in closing in on its quarry. It embarked upon extensive photographic surveillance, and planned its bombing raids from bases north of Paris and from airfields such as Vannes in North Western France.

The scene was set: the curtain was about to go up on a dramatic episode in the history of the town.

In the early days of the war, Swansea saw itself as a relatively quiet 'home front', but all that was about to change as the British Expeditionary Force was driven out of France at Dunkirk and the French capitulated. All too soon the town's population found itself in the terrifying conditions of a frontline war – the enemy was overhead and the town was under violent attack.

These wartime recollections are the memories of kids in that frontline war. Time has not dimmed their indelible images, nor their detailed recall of those wartime years that had such a dramatic effect on their young lives.

While much has been written about the devastation of the town and the experience of its adult population, the record regarding the observations and feelings of children is somewhat lighter. This is an attempt to add more weight to that record and to focus attention on the impact that war has on children.

After the German armed forces overran France, the children of Swansea were placed at the mercy of a terrifying and deadly enemy – an enemy who often struck when kids were at their most vulnerable – while sleeping. The first air raids on the town changed everything. The relative security of what was a distant home front quickly acquired the dangers and devastation of frontline war. Everything important to a child's feelings of security became an enemy target: home, family, pets, friends, playground and school. Nothing and nowhere was safe from the deadly rain of German bombs. In the fearful darkness of their blacked-out nights, Swansea children, like frightened rabbits, took to holes in the ground (Anderson Shelters) and the darkest recesses of their homes (cellars and dark cupboards under the stairs).

While the youngest had little comprehension of how the devastating effects of war were reshaping their daily lives, older children witnessed the disruptive and alarming destruction of their formerly secure worlds. Yet all was not doom and gloom. Children quickly adapted to these terrible times – even finding some measure of elation and pleasure in it all. Black nights of terror were offset with feelings of excitement. The spectacle of barrage balloons, ack-ack gunfire, blazing buildings and searchlights sweeping the night sky was enthralling. Morning-after air raids were charged with curiosity and eagerness to hunt out souvenirs.

The personal recollections that follow tell us something of childhoods disrupted by war. They give us insights and perceptions that only occasionally appear on the public record. Children who are victims of war, while being impressionable, are, all too often, silent observers – rarely do they have a public voice.

Seventy years on from the Second World War, this edition of *Frontline Kids* is an attempt to fill the gap.

It is the author's intention that on reading this story of Swansea in the years 1939 to 1945, from the point of view of children, it will go some way towards raising the awareness of us all about the vulnerability of children in war – all children in all wars.

As a way of introducing the wartime experiences of others, I shall begin with some of my own childhood recollections and experiences – fragmented in reality, but welded together here in a narrative that might be the story of any Swansea child of my age. I have also endeavoured to convey some of the atmosphere in which Swansea children found themselves in the early months of the 'Phoney War', when their home front life was relatively safe in a town that was not, as yet, fractured by barbaric conflict.

Regarding structure, the chapters are a series of themes that build into a graphic image of what it was like to be a child in Swansea in wartime. This is my way of encompassing everything that others have contributed to this work. I have made each chapter stand alone so readers can enter the narrative at any point.

Jim Owen
Sydney, Australia
June 2014

ACKNOWLEDGEMENTS

My thanks and appreciation to all those who provided material to enable me to compile this work: Graham Davies, Maureen Lewis, David Davies, Bernard Evans, Arthur Colburn, John Exall, Eric Wydenbach, Ken Gravelle, Joan Thomas, Alan Hughes, Sylvia Loveridge, John Lewis, Alan Davies, Peggy O'Neil Davies, Doreen Jones, Roger Jones, Michael Head, Alfred John Whitby, Neil Gordon, Cyril Gronert, and all those who contributed equally valuable material but who declined attribution.

My special thanks to Graham Davies for the wealth of contributions from himself and his friends, and for his sustained support throughout the development of this project. This is coupled with special thanks to Maureen Lewis for her encouragement and contributions.

My gratitude and thanks to Jeffrey Davies for his advice and input into the photographic material that appears in this book. Many thanks to the staff of the *South Wales Evening Post*, who were kind enough to publish my original request for email contributions to this work and for forwarding postal contributions. My special thanks to my brother, Brian Owen, for his contributions, encouragement and practical support.

Some material came to me second and third hand. I chose to include these pieces, as they were passed on to me by incorporating them into my narrative without paraphrasing them. I have treated unattributed material in the same way because it was so rich in personal expression and detail. My grateful thanks to you all.

PROLOGUE
EMERGING FROM THE FOG INTO WAR

Born in late 1938, I emerged from the fog of early childhood into a war I struggled to understand. In this I was not alone – there were many kids in Swansea like myself. Then there were slightly older children; children like my brother Brian – five at the outbreak of war – who, having only recently started school, had vivid pre-school memories and were now busy adjusting to their new school and war environments.

Kids like myself had not yet built solid memories sufficient to recall 'earlier times'. So as far as we were concerned, war (limited though our comprehension was) was the norm – taken for granted with all its fears and dreads.

It was the older children for whom memory became onerous, for it was they, like their adult counterparts, who remembered a more pleasant and peaceful life in pre-war Swansea – a peace and pace of life that was integral to their sense of stability. It was they who bore dreadful witness to their secure and familiar worlds being torn apart. It was they who suffered the enormous sense of loss with the Luftwaffe's destruction of their home town.

In my personal and gradually clearing childhood haze, wartime was a heady mixture of bewildering facts, unsolved mysteries, startling revelations, excitement, menace, terror, much happiness and a lot more besides. There were people sharing laughter about things that I didn't understand; there were women crying over things of which I knew nothing. In those early years, I just watched, uncomprehending, as the people around me went through a bewildering array of emotions – happy, sad, worried, tearful, terrified, nervous, elated and often angry – normal emotions but heightened and aggravated by the tensions of war. This, to me, was 'normal life', and I struggled to make sense of it all.

I had no problem in taking it all in. Making sense of it, however, was something else. I had absolutely no idea what war was about, but many times a day I was reminded that there was a war in progress when I heard such things as 'ah well, this won't win the war'; 'don't you know there's a war on'; 'before the war…' and 'when the war is over', which peppered everyone's everyday conversation. Undoubtedly, we were in the midst of war, whatever that was, and the all-pervading optimism was that we were inevitably going to win.

It seemed to me that in those days everybody sang or whistled as they went about their daily lives. I loved the sound of my mother singing while she was busy with household chores. She always seemed happy and full of promise. Lyrics like, 'There'll be bluebirds over the white cliffs of Dover … the valley will bloom again … tomorrow when the world is free' were always brimful of promise and hope. Songs like 'We'll

Meet Again', 'I'll Get By' and 'I'll Be Seeing You' lifted my young soul as I picked up on my mother's optimistic and propaganda-driven belief that all would come right in the end. These, it must be said, were powerful bonding forces in a crazy world.

My personal haze was penetrated by vivid experiences. I remember the awesome sight of searchlights criss-crossing the black night sky, the nights spent under the stairs with only a candle for light as my father stood 'watch' at the front door and in the street. I remember my mother's calming reassurances, though I also recall a profound and distinctly unnerving sense of fear. I remember long wailing sirens as we were snatched, half asleep, from our beds. I recall the panic-laced urgency as we took to our shelter.

Apart from these isolated experiences, which lodged in my developing memory, it was not until late 1942, when I was four years old, that things really began to fit into place. Up until that time things just accumulated in my head. Things memorised without the insight of reason and without any sense of chronology.

At the age of four, something just clicked. One day I woke up and found that suddenly I could tie up my own shoelaces. Out of the blue, the ability to reason somehow kicked in, and from that point on I was able, gradually, to make more sense of the devastation around me – much assisted by explanations from my brother, Brian, who was four-and-a-half years older. However personally enlightening as all this was, it didn't come with the grief and heartache that confronted older children. These children did it hard, harder than we might ever know. Their memory of how things used to be was still fresh, and completely at variance with the ever-present menace of air raids, a menace that disturbed their young minds and disrupted their developing lives.

For me, the disruption was normal. Being only nine months old at the outbreak of war, I knew nothing except war's disrupting effects on day-to-day life. This was how life was. I knew nothing of the centre of Swansea as a delightful pre-war mixture of shops, cafés, department stores, churches and dwellings. I knew nothing of the town that attracted great crowds from outlying districts, who considered a visit to Swansea a 'special day out'. To me the town centre was always a heap of rubble, in the midst of which, the Plaza Cinema, with its spellbinding ornate and gilded foyer, rose like a colossus out of the rubble. There were clearly defined roads through the debris (which I took for granted), but I was fascinated by the remnants of 'the market' – full of wooden stalls on its strangely uneven, scarred floor. The red-brick outer walls still stood defiant but I knew nothing of what they once contained. There was a heap of rubble at the end of St Helen's Road by the Hospital Square, which my mother pointed out as the place she used to bank, but that meant nothing to me. I saw it only as a heap of charred and fractured timbers sitting on a mound of broken bricks, though I was fascinated by papered walls with fireplaces stuck half way up the sides of adjoining premises.

For the people of Swansea, a heavily industrialized seaport town on the western seaboard of the British Isles, Thursday 14 June 1940 was just like any other day in those early months of the Second World War – unremarkable as days went. It was, however, a day that marked their destiny. A day when the unthinkable was set in train.

Apart from the grim news from the continent of the German war machine gaining momentum, there were few outward signs of major disruption to life in the town. Children went to school (though some had already been sent by their parents to the safety of the countryside), people went to work (though ever aware of the wartime measures now in place) and housewives did their shopping (albeit in an atmosphere of restrictions, rationing and queues). Buses and trains (though now curtailed in their services) routinely picked people up and dropped them off at their destinations, and industry hummed under a new impetus of the 'war effort'.

Swansea was a thriving industrial port. It boasted a newly built and award-winning Civic Centre, with its resplendent, modern, white stonework providing a striking contrast with the buildings of the old town centre, huddled as they were around the docks and the remnants of the town's Norman castle. The clock tower of the new Civic Centre was an impressive and unmistakable landmark (especially by day for low flying German bombers), a fact that would play heavily on the fears on some children who lived nearby. The market, too, was an outstanding landmark, with its great glassed roof. A focal point for shoppers and vendors from far and wide, this great hall was as busy as ever that morning. For department stores and a whole host of smaller shops, it was more or less business as usual (though under 'Phoney War' conditions) and, for many of the town's traders and shoppers, nothing of what they heard on the wireless that day (momentous though it was) interrupted their routine. Typically, the Davies family (well-known bakers in Nelson Street who supplied a steady stream of customers trekking between the Market and the Singleton Street bus station) took the day's news in its stride. France had fallen – it was to be expected.

The news had never been good since the outbreak of war nearly nine months earlier, and the Fall of France, close on the heels of the routing of the British Expeditionary Force at Dunkirk, with its amazingly small loss of life, seemed just another bit of bad news. Serious though the capitulation of the French was, somehow it all appeared to be far distant and not too much of a threat to the people of Swansea. After all, how much better off were they than the English who had a mere 22 miles between them and the German forces at the Straits of Dover? All would be well … or so it seemed.

For Swansea's population, on that fateful Thursday in June 1940, the war was not yet a tragedy and there was little anticipation of what was to come. The reality was, however, that the powerful forces of the Third Reich were positioned to strike. The town's fate was sealed. The machinery was set in motion for the destruction of Swansea.

There was some speculative talk about air raids, as there had been when the blackout was introduced at the outbreak of the war, but this was generally dismissed. There was also a lot of talk about a possible German invasion. This was further fueled by precautions put in place by the authorities. Anti-invasion defences were installed on the beaches and people were 'put on their guard', but all these threats were soon smothered in the prevailing optimism, generated partly by the lighter side of propaganda and partly in the belief that it couldn't happen to Swansea. While the thought of invasion and air attacks struck fear into everyone, somehow people were able to make light of it all.

Apart from the heartache that accompanied mobilisation of the husbands, fathers, boyfriends, sons and brothers; the imposition of the 'blackout'; the direction of many women into war related employment and wartime measures in place everywhere, there was, outwardly, little change to be seen on the home front. So despite the sombre commentary from the BBC on the Fall of France, its consequences for Swansea seemed, on the surface, to be greatly underestimated by the great majority of its townsfolk, who were anticipating the enjoyment of the coming summer, as they had with all summers that had gone before.

As France was overrun, the Luftwaffe quickly took over the airport at Vannes – a costal town in North West France – and immediately commenced upgrading the facilities to accommodate fighter and bomber operations. This was to be one of the bases from which bombing attacks were to be launched on Swansea. Plans for the aerial surveillance of large areas of Wales were well advanced by German aircrews based north of Paris. All was in readiness to menace and unsettle the population of Swansea.

At 3.30 a.m. on 27 June 1940, the Luftwaffe struck its first blow. While Swansea slept, the first bombs fell on Danygraig Road and Kilvey Hill. Swansea kids were now in the front line of war, a war they would find terrifying, spectacular, sometimes exciting, often deadly and always memorable.

This is Swansea Market today, rebuilt on the site laid waste by intensive Luftwaffe bombing. Once a great glass and steel structure, supported on stout, red-brick walls, you would enter on this Oxford Street side through a great, majestic two-towered gateway. The same entrance is harder to find today, but, once inside, Swansea market has recaptured its former reputation as one of the country's finest markets for fresh food and local products. In years gone by, kids loved it.

1

WARTIME CHILDHOOD: MENACING, EXCITING, MEMORABLE

The following recollections, from a diverse range of sources, provide glimpses of Swansea children at home, school and play during the war years. Together they build a picture of how the war disrupted their routines; how it influenced children's fantasies and their play; the games they played; the things that troubled them; the intrusions of war that influenced and shaped their young lives. The detail and the candour of these recollections, besides displaying strong and enduring connections between the erstwhile child and the present day adult, provide a rich tapestry of information about childhood in the dark years of our recent history.

School Days

Peggy O'Neil Davies describes how the war disrupted her school days, forcing kids out of the classroom and changing the way their lessons were conducted. She reminds us of the hurdles teachers faced in helping youngsters learn under difficult circumstances.

We weren't able to concentrate. Some few months after the war started, the air raids started on Swansea – not very much in the beginning. We had to have cushions made of rubber pads (by our mothers) to take to school, so that when the air-raid sirens went we would take our cushions and sit on the stairs. At first, the teachers tried to teach the lessons, but as a lot of us were squashed together on each stair it was decided we weren't able to concentrate so we used to have stories read to us. We also sang songs or recited poetry.

When the sirens sounded more often, and the bombing became worse, it was decided that we should run home. If your home was too far away you went with someone who lived near the school. If the sirens went in the night we didn't have to go to school until eleven o'clock, as we all had to get up in the night and go into shelters. By this time a lot of houses had air-raid shelters built into the ground in their gardens.

Graham Davies relates how his schooldays were disrupted and the effect that war had on the Secondary School curriculum.

In 1944 I went to Dynevor Grammar School, which was in a sad state of repair having been damaged in the Blitz. Also, there was a shortage of teachers in certain specialist subjects. Our nights were filled with fears, but the mornings were exciting. We had been awake for most of the night so school was cancelled. Normal routine was completely disturbed. We had breakfast at 6.00 a.m. when Dad came home from fire watching. More important – there was no school.

Others recalled how the bombing affected their trips to school by bus.

Our school, St David's, was in the centre of town. Sometimes we didn't get to school until late because there was a bomb crater in the middle of a road where the bus usually went. The driver would have to go all around the back streets. Sometimes the road was blocked with fire hoses and fire engines. The hoses snaked everywhere and they always had leaks – small holes in the hose that sprayed water everywhere.

On one occasion, when we were going home from school, the bus was turned back because there was an unexploded bomb in a butcher's shop by the Hospital Square. It must have been there when we went to school that way in the morning, but nobody knew about it.

MAKE-BELIEVE WAR GAMES

After the Fall of France, talk of a German invasion was widespread. Children picked up on such things and incorporated them into their play. As a child, Arthur Colburn lived in Port Talbot. His recollections of the war's influence on his childhood games underscores the extent to which the war dominated children's thinking and infiltrated their play.

Arthur Colburn recalls,

It was decided to build a submarine at the back of Davies the dairy. As a result of the threat of the German invasion, the Home Guard were carrying out exercises in the town. They concentrated on the bridge over the River Avon near Bethany Square, which carried the main London road. They set up their sandbags outside Bert Willsher's tobacconist and newspaper shop every Sunday morning. We kids couldn't understand why the Germans planned to come down Pentyla Hill on a Sunday morning, but decided that these old guys, for indeed they looked quite old to us, needed some help.

   A defence force was set up to replace what used to be known, before the war, as the Black Hand Gang – all three of us taking it in turns to be the commanding officer.

   In Forge Road, the high command of the defence force heard that the Atlantic convoys were being attacked, and so it was decided to build a submarine. The naval base was the garage at the back of Davies the dairy, which was owned by my friend

Ronnie's family. His dad, Ray, was an officer in the Royal Air Force. Ronnie was the second member of our high command and lived next door to me.

The submarine consisted of my father's ladder, supported by two oil drums and covered with potato sacks, on loan from Bowden's fruit and veg' store. This was owned by Graham's family and he was the third member of our high command. His older brother, Peter, was serving in the RAF, but, tragically, his plane came down in France in 1940 and he was killed. He had been a peacetime flier, joining the RAF after leaving the grammar school before the war.

Arthur continues recounting the death of his friend's brother.

It was after a bombing mission over Dusseldorf that his Sterling bomber had crashed, and he and the rest of the crew lost their lives. They were buried at a small village in France called Souanne.

We three courageous adventurers roamed the high seas in our submarine, often under attack from Stukas and U-boats, but we always managed to be back in time for tea. There were times, however, when we were refuelled, at sea, by Mrs Davies, with glasses of Corona pop, served out of those bottles with a wire clip top.

Out on patrol, at the command 'Up Periscope', a broom head would emerge through an opening in the rungs of the ladder. This was followed by the small head of the look-out. At any sign of danger, he would shout 'dive, dive, dive!', and we would batten down all the sacking and descend into the deep to await the depth charges. If we were hit, we would carefully look for leaks with our torch.

Our communication network with our base was a tight piece of string between two cocoa tins. After Pearl Harbour, we added extra fuel tanks (another oil drum from the garage), and we spent long hours in the Pacific looking for the Japanese. Our families had no idea how far we travelled or what we had to face on those extremely dangerous assignments.

STREET GAMES

With the outbreak of war, the use of private civilian cars was severely restricted and suburban streets went quiet. This was a great bonus for kids. They took possession of the streets all over town and made the centre of the road their playground. Apart from the occasional vehicle, street cricket and football games went uninterrupted – but not without upsetting a neighbour or two. One of these children recalled, 'As kids we felt the street belonged to us. Adults had houses but the street was ours.'

Grumpy neighbours – every street had them! We had Mrs Harris and Mrs Ward. They were always grumpy and always wanted us to 'go and play somewhere else', sometimes with good cause (broken windows were hard to replace in wartime), but we were just kids having fun and making a noise. Whenever the ball was withheld with the threat of confiscation, we would always stop and listen with feigned respect – otherwise we wouldn't get the ball back!

Both Mrs Harris and Mrs Ward must have been thankful for the long, blacked-out winter nights when it got dark early and the kids were off the streets, but, no doubt, they didn't care much for double British summer time when the weather was fine and it didn't get dark until nearly eleven o'clock.

Sometimes games were forcibly stopped by irate neighbours hell-bent on protecting prized possessions like hedges, flower gardens and, of course, windows. Kids being kids, they sometimes got carried away – inclined to be unthinking and a bit destructive.

Wartime for kids was the golden age of utility.

Marbles were popular, and collections, all pre-war, were prized. However, with wartime scarcity everything became 'hand-me-down' and 'utility' was everything. Cosseted marble collections took to the gutters everywhere. Fewer parked cars meant great stretches of gutters in which to play an uninterrupted game of 'allies' – as marbles were known.

Other collectables:

There was also a very popular game played with cigarette cards and later with round cardboard milk bottle tops.

More street games:

Pavements and streets everywhere were chalked-up for games of hopscotch – a hop-and-step game usually played by girls. Bombed sites became a great source of chunks of plaster, for 'chalking' out the lines, and a glazed bit of a broken kitchen sink made an ideal 'pitch' for accurate sliding into a designated square. Skipping, using a long piece of rope, was also very popular with girls.

Not all street games were boisterous.

The games of 'I-spy' and 'film stars' were great favourites. Everybody trundled out the old stalwart 'ZP', though I doubt if any kid who played 'Film Stars' ever knew what Zazzu Pitts looked like, let alone see her films … if it was a 'her'

Determining who would have the first 'go' was a game in itself.

'Eenie, meanie miney mo' was in every child's repertoire to get games started. Another was 'Smooth the white rabbit'.'

Most of these street games continued for many years into the peace, but there were some street activities that came to an abrupt end with the end of the war.

SOUVENIR HUNTING

Graham Davies lived opposite the Civic Centre and, like many wartime kids, he developed a keen interest in collecting fragments from exploded bombs and ack-ack gun shells.

> Children of our age had a new craze – looking for shrapnel. Charred green incendiary fins and burnt out flares were easily found on the greens opposite (on the lawns of the Civic Centre). The prized 'find' was a piece of German shrapnel.

After one raid, when we were looking for shrapnel the next morning (even though I knew what shrapnel looked like I didn't have a clue where it came from, but I knew it was something to collect), I remember the cricket field gate was wide open and the field was littered with white bombs that I was told were unexploded incendiaries. Soldiers stopped us from taking a closer look.'

THE BEACH

When the threat of an invasion loomed, access to the beach was restricted. However, the beach wasn't out of bounds for the entire 'duration'. For those kids lucky enough to have the beach as an alternative playground to the street, a favourite game was to build a fleet of ships out of sand. The addition of twigs, stones and anything else that helped identify a roughly fashioned hull as a battle cruiser, armed merchantman or whatever, was as much a part of the game as what followed.

> We would spend ages building a convoy of ships out of sand and anything else we could find. We'd then have three stones each – as large as you were able to throw – to bombard the convoy from some distance away. We'd then inspect the damage caused by our own stones.

> My sisters would build sandcastles and decorate them with all sorts of shells and small stones. I thought sandcastles were 'sissy'. I much preferred to build a huge German battleship and then 'bomb' it from a distance with big stones. My mother was always calling out, 'Watch where you're throwing those stones. Someone will get hurt.' The main object of my game was to land a direct hit on the ship's magazine. That didn't happen often, so it was a matter of seeing how many throws it took to cause enough damage to declare it 'sunk'.
>
> Sometimes my mother took me to the beach after school on summer evenings and we'd have our tea there. Soggy tomato sandwiches gritty with sand were a feature of my wartime summers at the beach.

The beach could also be a hazardous playground.

> We were on the beach on a hot summer's day and went swimming in the incoming tide. The sea was covered in oil and so were my friend and I. There was wreckage everywhere. Hatches, drums etc., all coming in on the tide. A ship had been mined in the Channel. We had great difficulty getting the oil and tar off our skin.

Swansea beach in peacetime. During the war there was a variety of anti-invasion seafront arrangements. Machine gun posts, oiled and tarred defences ready for torching (in the event of enemy troop landings) and a spectacular array of anti-landing craft defences, which stretched for miles below the high tide mark, together with heavily guarded access points, kept the sands strictly off limits.

WEAR AND TEAR

Clothes were rationed but people were resourceful. The following recollections give us some idea of what kids wore, and the trouble that parents went to in making clothes last.

During the war, what kids wore everyday, in and out of school, was a matter of 'make-do-and-mend', as people used to say. New clothes were referred to as 'Sunday Best' and were only worn on high days and holidays.

Everything woollen was worn until it was threadbare or went into holes – then it was 'darned'. Mothers would spend evenings darning clothes to be worn next day. Everyone wore woollen pullovers, jumpers, socks, and gloves that required regular darning – clothes were rationed so nothing was thrown out. I can still picture my mother with her hand in a sock, which had a hole in it, darning away listening to the radio.

My father had a cobbler's last and was often found 'tapping' (repairing) our shoes. Like lots of other kids, we'd have the soles of our shoes covered in studs to save the leather. Our shoes weighed a ton and were very noisy when we walked. But studs were great. We used to have competitions to see who could produce the most sparks when we kicked our shoes hard against the rough surface of the road or pavement.

Nearly everything I wore was a hand-me-down. I can't remember wearing anything to school that wasn't repaired. My trousers were patched; my shirt collars turned; my socks and pullover were darned. I looked like a regular little urchin when I had my basin haircut. The basin cut looked like the barber had put a pudding basin over your head to cut your hair. It left you with a shock of hair on top, and a line around your head, below which you were close-cropped to the skin, but after a day or so it didn't look too bad.

I remember heavy woollen 'bathers' that always sagged under the weight of water. Woollen bathers were the standard swimwear for men and boys. Girl's bathers were made out of elasticated cotton with lots of weird stitching.

WARTIME SMELLS

Brian Owen recalls,

Nothing went to waste in wartime. Under the lamp-post outside Mrs Scott's (she ran the fish and chip shop in Francis Street round the corner from St Helen's Avenue) was a 'pig bin' where people put all their vegetable waste – potato peelings, cabbage stumps etc. An old man with a horse and cart collected the stuff and took it somewhere to feed the pigs. As you can guess, the smell from the bin on some days was awful – no wonder pig meat was prone to give you an upset stomach.

Life was a struggle when it came to feeding families, but some things weren't on ration and many families made stews from sheep, pig and calves' heads. One wartime child still has vivid recollections of things we ate.

The smell of dampened dust, burnt wood and charred bricks evokes memories of bomb damaged houses for children who, despite the dangers and repeated warnings, found play among the tangled rubble of bombed buildings exciting. For many, the smell of burning candles evokes wartime memories of nights huddled in the shelter of dark places.

St Helen's Avenue post-war. Gone are those wartime chalked-up hopscotch pitches, the kids playing in the middle of the road and those awful smelling 'pig bins'. Houses are now brighter and 'done up'. Wartime hedges, which filled the gaps from removed iron railings, have given way to walls. Neighbours are rarely seen, let alone heard. To a wartime kid, the place has lost its atmosphere.

Michael Head recalls nights in Skewen when he was three or four years old.

It is the smell of domestic candles that whizzes me back to our shelter in the garden. When the bombing of the Swansea Oil Refinery was at its most persistent, we spent long periods of the night as a family in the shelter, lit by candles that gave off a comforting musky, waxy smell. It was never frightening because I was sure we were going to win the war. My dad said that and I knew he was right. Having my dad and mum together, with my sister and I, was unusual and exciting. My dad worked long hours in the Mond Nickel Company. He left the house before we were up in the morning and often returned just as we were going to bed.

Having both of them with us for long periods gave us a powerful sense of family – its 'fourness' and completeness. No agendas, just passing the night until the all clear. My dad always told us stories from his own real childhood, or from the films that he occasionally saw on his own. In the morning after the all-clear, there was no appearance of disaster – our house was there and we went back to bed until the normal day began.

FEARS & NIGHTMARES

The first three air raids on Swansea, beginning on 27 June 1940, were to have a profound effect on children. Vivid imaginations stoked kids' fears and there was little that adults, themselves terrified, could say or do to reassure them. The fears of older children may well have been heightened by what they knew of the bombing of Warsaw and the earlier German bombing raids on Spanish towns during the Spanish Civil War.

SOUNDS FAMILIAR

No warning was given before these first three air attacks, a fact that added greatly to everyone's anxiety. Kids became stressed in anticipation of further surprise attacks. That anticipation fanned their fears – so much so that when the air-raid sirens did finally sound, kids became terrified. The baleful whining of the siren itself triggered distress in some children.

Brian Owen remembers,

The first time I heard the air-raid siren I cried. I remember a terrible feeling of fear and dread, picked up, no doubt from the reaction and conversation of the adults around me. This never really left me, though, as time went by I got used to it.'

Fear came from everywhere. Even the simple routine of putting on a gas mask was terrifying for some kids and caused great anxiety for others. After being told of the dire consequences of not wearing a gas mask, I became very fearful and constantly worried about Stella, our Scottish Terrier – Stella didn't have a gas mask! What would happen to her? I loved dogs. Every time I heard an air-raid siren and saw my gas mask 'at the ready'. I hugged Stella because I thought she was going to die. Children's imaginations also went into overdrive thinking of the possible consequences of bombing.

Graham Davies recalls one of his fears.

It was my secret fear. A chilling thought of a direct hit from a German bomber onto the Civic Centre directly opposite to our house in the Crescent. The clock tower would shudder and then come toppling down across the Civic greens like a big white wave destroying our house. Or perhaps the tower would fall short or tumble the other way into Victoria Park. Such were the fears of an 8-year-old in Swansea in February 1941. Just to the left of the main entrance to the Civic Centre was a bomb crater. There was another on the steps of the Brangwyn Hall. My secret fear had nearly happened.

A 'montage of menace'. Kids who witnessed a low-flying Heinkel fighter bomber, suddenly appearing out of the blue, were both terrified and awestruck by these powerful and deadly war machines.

Brian Owen also recalls the same bomb crater outside the Brangwyn Hall.

> I remember standing on the edge of the crater and looking down. It was quite deep. There didn't appear to be any damage to the building itself. The blast must have gone in another direction.

The white stone tower of the Civic Centre, both a conspicious landmark and a bombing target feared by local kids, narrowly escaped a direct hit by a bomb, which landed on the steps of the Brangwyn Hall.

The pitch-blackness of the night sky, though a source of terror, was also a place of wonderment and endless fascination for many.

Brian Owen recollects the spectacle of it all.

> I have memories of searchlights. I loved the display as they swept the sky and lit up the clouds. You could see the light travel from the source into the atmosphere. Sometimes three or more would intersect. It was like a firework display. I can't ever remember seeing an aircraft caught in the beams.

Graham Davies recalls the BBC newsreaders Alvar Liddell and Bruce Belfrage, who became household names during wartime. Alvar Liddel, whose authoritative and assuring voice was as familiar to me as anyone of the family, read the one o'clock news. Although I didn't comprehend what he said, I got the feeling of it being 'good' or 'bad' from the reaction of my mother, who sometimes commented on the news we were hearing.

WARTIME SAYINGS & SLOGANS

There were many sayings that were with us for the duration of the war and then disappeared as soon as it was over. Among these were some already mentioned, like 'Don't you know there's a war on', and 'Ah well, this won't win the war', which usually terminated a tea break or a bit of 'chin wag'. There were other well-worn sayings that were particular to certain families.

Alan Hughes recalls,

> The following are two most memorable sayings from that time – words spoken to me by parents. I must have been making a noise when my mother said, 'Shush Al, I am listening to the news to hear if Hitler is coming.' From another time, I can still hear Dad's voice at the dining table: 'You don't spread marg – you scrape it on your bread'. 'Lick the plate if you're hungry' was a great excuse for bad manners, and much quoted by kids.

Not in the category of a 'much repeated' saying, but nevertheless memorable for one Sandfields boy, was one his mother came out with one day. She was frying sausages for her son's dinner while listening to Lord Haw Haw broadcasting German propaganda with his impeccable English accent. With the aim of demoralizing those who listened, Lord Haw Haw was 'ranting on' about how the British were starving – at which the mother thrust the frying pan at the wireless and said 'Starving are we Lord bloody Haw Haw – well smell that!'

Slogans were a feature of life in wartime. They were short, easy to remember and sent powerful messages to the population. They usually presented themselves on posters, conveying both a strong visual image and a forceful message. In the main, slogans focused on matters of health and wartime precautions, like 'Coughs and Sneezes spread diseases', and the one that Arthur Colburn recollects,which inhibited the spreading of information that might be useful to enemy spies: 'Careless talk costs lives.'

Arthur Colburn remembers this wartime slogan and recalls how fact and fantasy merged into one to become a memorable adventure for a bunch of kids from Port Talbot.

> We had a real life adventure. While walking up Baglan Mountain, we found a dead pigeon with a tiny canister fixed to its leg. Posters pasted to walls around Port Talbot during the war stated 'Careless talk costs lives'. Quite clearly the pigeon that we had found, with its secret message, proved that someone had been talking!

Arthur's story serves to remind us of the impact that propaganda had on kids. Its influence in blurring childhood fantasy and reality is plain to see.

'WALES NEEDS HOME RULE NOT WAR'

This was one slogan that, although unofficial, was prominently placed and carried a powerful and heartfelt message for some. It was painted in large white letters on the brick wall of the Cricket Field opposite the Patti Pavilion. Everybody heading for Mumbles on the Mumbles Road during the war, and for some considerable time afterwards, would have read it. Every time I passed it I read it aloud. I was too young to understand what it meant but I recall it was the first sentence I ever read.

In spite of the blitz and the privations of war, people still found ways of enjoying themselves. Cinema boomed and dancing was very popular – especially dancing on Saturday nights. Everybody, or so it seemed, from far and wide, spent time walking on 'the prom'. It was the place to meet people. Parks were full, likewise cafés. War, when it wasn't inflicting tragedy, introduced an element of romance. People found the spirit of friendship, that came with the times, made it easier to meet a broader cross-section of people. There was no shortage of people falling in love – even before the Americans arrived! This could cause family friction.

> Some of the kids we knew had older sisters who were always having rows with their parents. These rows were always about make-up, boyfriends and the amount of time spent 'gallivanting'. One kid told us how his father had locked his sister in her bedroom but she escaped, by climbing down a drainpipe, and went dancing with her girlfriend from next door. There were ructions when she eventually got home.

A HOLIDAY AND HASTY RETREAT

Despite the war, some were lucky enough to get away on holiday – even it were only to visit relatives in London. However, such holidays were also full of perils. The excitement of one youngster's first trip to London was soon 'dampened' by the incessant howling of a demanding baby cousin. But merciful relief was at hand (courtesy of Hitler) with the arrival of the first doodlebug and a hurried return home.

DIGGING FOR VICTORY – ON SOMEONE ELSE'S CABBAGE PATCH!

There were allotments everywhere. These highly productive patches of land were a satisfying hobby for many, and very rewarding – if you got in before the poachers!

Kids were everywhere and saw everything, including poachers returning home just before dark carrying bags laden with fresh vegetables. Often the 'booty' was shared in exchange for keeping quiet.

'SINISTER GOINGS-ON'

Some kids recalled 'sinister goings-on', but details are scarce. The 'Black Market', suspicious activity, unexplained hostility between neighbours and strange 'Pig Societies' headed the list of sinister elements of life in wartime, the details of which were largely denied to kids, thus keeping these 'goings on' adult secrets.

The Slip bridge, now dismantled, with the steelwork forming part of the pathway on the prom, was a landmark which many people held dear. Wartime kids loved it and many played there when the beach was reopened to the public. It did have its hair-raising moments. Always a marvellous vantage point for watching the Mumbles train and the steam trains coming and going.

2

DEFENCES – AS KIDS SAW THEM

Wartime defences held much interest, excitement and terror for children. The spectacle of barrage balloons, like great lumbering elephants in the sky, was always a cause of great interest and excitement. There was much that terrified kids in wartime. For those who were naturally afraid of the dark, the blacked-out nights were an ordeal. Gas masks too caused their share of distress. Not only did they induce feelings of claustrophobia for some, but they often caused young children to scream in terror when their mother's friendly face was dramatically transformed while wearing one.

For those who understood the implications of enemy invasion, the sight of invasion defences were sometimes of little comfort. While offering some reassurance about keeping an enemy out, they were also capable of striking a note of terror in fertile young imaginations when they explored ways in which the enemy might overcome them. 'What if?' and 'then what?' were questions that often went unanswered, leaving children heavily burdened with fears generated by their own vivid imaginations.

Searchlights silently prowling the black night sky, though sinister, never failed to fascinate. Defensive ack-ack gunfire was both noisily terrifying and enthralling to watch. Children found sandbags fun to play on; the idea of bomber decoys (a defensive strategy to mislead the enemy) fired imaginations. For a few kids living in St Helen's Avenue, an incendiary bomb 'catching device' proved a source of entertainment when it wasn't doing its job.

BOMBER DECOYS
On an isolated part of Fairwood Common, on the opposite side to Nazareth House, was a fire decoy site. Drums of oil were stored on this relatively remote part of the common to be set alight during a raid, to fool German bomber pilots. This decoy was never set on fire in an effort to draw bombers away from the town at night but was ignited one afternoon – struck by lightening during a storm!

Thinking that a bomb had hit Nazareth House, everyone from the bungalows in the fields around Murton descended on the scene to help, only to find the decoy ablaze and gorse fires racing across the common.

Propaganda: Strengthening Mental Defences

Propaganda played its part in providing a measure of defence against grim reality. Cynical adults might have been able to balance the excesses of propaganda with common sense, but, by and large, propaganda worked well on children. Kids often accepted it as fact without question. Anything that belittled the power and strength of the enemy and its leaders was pressed into service, and was well received. Propaganda sometimes fed us with preposterous, and unfortunately, enduring notions. There weren't any official posters proclaiming 'the only good German was a dead one', but the saying was widespread and readily entered the culture of children. The saying became integral to their view of the world and persisted for many years after hostilities had ceased.

Propaganda was an important way of strengthening our mental defences. In some cases, it worked by trivialising menace. Kids everywhere would mimic comedians in their ridicule of the German and Italian leaders.

Graham Davies recalls that

> Adolf Hitler and Benito Mussolini were presented as figures of fun – Adolf jackbooted with a funny little moustache and Benito a plump, puffed-up dictator who made funny gestures and assumed comic poses.

Comedians such as Tommy Trinder, Tommy Handley, Max Miller, Flanagan and Allen and George Formby did much for the cause. Mocking Hitler was a great source of fun for radio, film and music hall audiences and a sure fire way to raise a laugh.

Graham continued,

> In one of his films, George Formby, ever the unlikely hero but a great favourite with kids, captured German spies. Conrad Veidt (an actor in British films) specialised in focusing our hate on the sinister German U-Boat commander he played to perfection.

Music stirred our patriotic emotions. The words of songs were reassuring. Designed to make people feel good, they invariably hit their mark.

Brian Owen remembers,

> Propaganda worked on me because I always felt happy when songs like 'When They Sound the Last All Clear' came on the wireless.

Every kid fell for the fact that eating carrots would make them able to see in the dark – it worked for rabbits! This brings us to the blackout. None of us could eat enough carrots to be able to penetrate the frightening ink-blackness of some wartime nights. There were many other propaganda exercises that caught the imaginations of children.

Brian recalls a very special bomb in 1943.

> A bomb casing was displayed in the Market and people were invited to stick savings stamps all over it. This propaganda exercise was very popular with kids – I could hardly wait to make my contribution. This was a way of personalizing people's involvement with bombing reprisals, by getting them to identify with, and to pay for, a particular bomb.

Brian added,

> Bomber Harris (Commander of the British Bombing Squadrons) did the rest, but with such a heavy loss of allied aircraft and aircrew lives that the exercise became prohibitive. But, of course, the public didn't know this at the time. Censorship worked hand in glove with propaganda.
>
> The bomb case was about the height of a six-year-old child. The gimmick was to get people to buy stamps (savings stamps) to stick all over it. The bomb was later dropped as a 500 lb load of high explosive on the enemy – no doubt maiming and killing children like ourselves, but this never really crossed our minds as propaganda focused us on thinking of the enemy in terms of fighting men and the machinery of war.
>
> Sticking stamps on bombs was a successful propaganda exercise that earned the post office a substantial profit. A uniformed post official was always in attendance with sheets of stamps to sell, while the children were organized to step forward, one at a time, for their moment in the spotlight.

Brian recalls another propaganda exercise.

> Propagandists placed a 'downed' Messerschmidt fighter, where people could see and touch it and feel pride in the damaged prize – now out of harm-causing way for the duration. People marveled at the sight and were spurred on to join National Savings to 'save for victory'.

SANDBAGS AND SEARCHLIGHTS

Searchlights and sandbags are enduring icons of the Second World War. Wherever you went there were sandbags. Small, fat and often damp, these sacking bags filled with sand were stacked neatly against important buildings. They served to protect the lower parts of buildings against bomb blast.

Graham Davies recalls them

> ...piled about three high around the Civic Centre whose windows were all taped with white crosses – more blast protection.

'Searchlights in the Cricket Field', sketched from memory by Brian Owen. Kids were fascinated by the spectacular displays.

Brian Owen recollects a moment of embarrassment involving sandbags.

> There were sandbags to be found everywhere. As a kid I loved to walk on them –
> especially the ones around the Civic Centre. One day a policeman caught me and 'tore
> me off a strip'. I felt awful.

Close up, or at a distance, searchlights were a fascinating spectacle as they swept the
sky for enemy aircraft. Their displays were brilliant against the blackness of wartime
night skies, and despite the fact that it was dangerous (due to falling shrapnel and
bombs) for anyone to be away from shelter while these powerful lights were searching
out their targets, many took the risk. Such spectacles were pure magic to kids.

THE BLACKOUT

A rigorously maintained defence against night attacks was the blackout, one of the great
hallmarks of the Second World War home front. Put in place at the declaration of war
in September 1939, in the anticipation night air attacks, the blackout was maintained
until 1945. For Swansea kids, used to playing by the light of street lamps, the pitch-black
nights not only curtailed their play but also brought terror into their lives.

The pitch-black night held a peculiar sense of terror for me – you just never knew
who or what was out there. Moonlit nights were a great bonus and a welcome relief
from the total darkness, yet total darkness was both exciting and terrifying. Torches
dimmed and pointed at our feet to light the ground beneath us always made a
necessary night walk exciting, but I always remember having a fright whenever we
passed someone, who, out of the darkness, alerted you to their presence with a sudden,
detached 'goodnight', or a 'keep that torch down' from an unseen ARP warden.

Some nights we went to see Mrs Perry, Mam's friend, and her daughter, Dorothy,
who was a few years older than myself. They lived around the corner on King Edwards
Road. We'd spend evenings doing jigsaws (over which everyone chatted). We always
finished up the evening with cups of tea and meat paste sandwiches.

THE DREADED TELEGRAM

Mrs Perry had two sons in the Army. I always remember her saying to my mother that
she lived in fear of getting a telegram. I was too young to understand why and nobody
gave me an answer but young as I was I knew that everyone lived in fear of a telegram – a
fear against which there was no defence.

I have enduring memories of leaving Mrs Perry's house in the pitch darkness. It was
so dark I couldn't see my mother standing beside me, I could only hear her voice and
searched the darkness for her hand to hold. When it was wet and windy, the walk home
was an ordeal. If we didn't have a torch we invariably misjudged where the puddles
were and got wet feet. I always found total darkness unsettling, especially at home in the
minutes before the candles were lit – something that seemed to happen often back then.
I remember we had heavy velvet curtains on our windows and a blanket hung over the

back door to stop any light escaping when someone went to get coal for the fire. I recall the ARP man in the street calling out to 'put that light out' when someone carelessly put a light on without first drawing the curtains.

I also have recollections of the following story, much repeated by my parents during the war, about a man who lived in the flats on the corner of St Helens Avenue and Gorse Lane. I remember him as being very sullen and of 'foreign' appearance. We often saw him while we played in the street. He lived in the second-floor flat, which had a large bay window that overlooked the cricket field and had a clear view to Mumbles Head and across the Bristol Channel.

I remember my father saying that the ARP warden was always knocking on his door shouting 'put that light out' because he would have a light on with the curtains not drawn. The man always claimed he had fallen asleep with a light on and didn't wake up until after it got dark. Then, one day, he left his flat in the afternoon and didn't return before dark – leaving a light on and his curtains wide open. The soldiers garrisoned in the Cricket Field, on finding this well-lit bay window presenting a perfect beacon for any enemy aircraft coming up the Channel, shot out the light with a rifle. Next day, the man was taken away by the police. Nobody knew what happened to him. He never returned to the flat, which, soon afterwards, was occupied by a family.

BARRAGE BALLOONS
Brian Owen recalls,

> Barrage balloons were used to deter attack from low-flying aircraft. There was a barrage balloon site at the top end of Victoria Park next to the Civic Centre. The balloon was attached to a truck, from which it was winched into position. Cables and the voluminous presence of this balloon – like a large, sky-borne, lumbering elephant – were used as a defence against low-flying German bombers.
>
> Ships were often seen leaving the docks and heading out to sea towing balloons for protection against dive-bomber attacks. The Patti Pavilion, in Victoria Park, was used for barrage balloon maintenance.

One day the barrage balloon moored in the park collapsed and came crashing down on the beach by Swansea Bay station. It must have been during the summer because I remember there were a lot of people sitting on the beach. Soon, the balloon was surrounded by people trying to tear it apart. Some mothers told their kids to run home and fetch some scissors – presumably because they had a use for the silvery fabric. However, soldiers from the park soon arrived and stopped people causing more damage.

THE INCENDIARY CATCHER
Ever the inventor, **Len Owen** devised a way of dealing with firebombs. These bombs were the cause of much destruction. Their ability to pierce the roof of a house and

ignite would invariably mean the loss of the home – unless they could be picked up safely, and deposited out of harm's way. Len's invention could do just that.

Brian recollects that

> Incendiary bombs were a menace. They fell everywhere causing havoc. My father invented a 'catcher' for dealing with burning bombs. It was a metal case, lined with asbestos, which could be opened and closed, like a set of jaws, by a pull chord that ran up the length of the broom handle to which the metal case was attached.

I'm not sure if it worked effectively in scooping up firebombs, but us kids had great fun seeing if we could catch a ball with it, or seeing if we were faster than the one pulling the chord trying to trap our hand or foot. I can remember that for years after the war it was kept in the outside toilet behind the door, where it was an awkward nuisance.

GAS MASKS

Everyone was issued with a gas mask and was expected to carry it with them everywhere. It was a common sight to see people with their brown cardboard gas mask box slung over their shoulders on a long loop of string. Too small for gas masks, infants were placed in individual tent-like devices fitted with an observation panel and a hand pump, with which the mother was able to keep the infant alive. Most wartime children remember feelings of claustrophobia when wearing their gas masks.

Sylvia Loveridge remembers,

> Gas-masks were awful to wear and we had to take them with us wherever we went. There were baby ones, Mickey Mouse ones and grown-up ones, and they were all horrible. We also had to remember our identity numbers as well. Mine is implanted in my brain to this day.

Peggy O'Neil Davies recalls that

> Everyone was issued with a gas mask, a ration book, sweet coupons and coupons for clothes. Wherever we went we had to take our gas masks. Every week in school we had to put on these gas masks, which wasn't very nice. The teacher placed a piece of paper on every child's desk and we had to pick it up with the mask on to show we were breathing properly – the paper had to stay on the end. We often did our lessons wearing these masks. It was in case a gas bomb dropped.

ACK-ACK GUNS

Alan Hughes recollects some of the ack-ack gun positions.

The Cricket Field, Ashleigh Road and other sites all over town (Llandarcy oil refinery etc..). Numbers of people manning them. The spectacle, especially when combined with searchlights (as in the cricket field).

During an air raid and bombing, the ack-ack (local anti aircraft guns 3' to 4' caliber) would blast off. The shells exploded causing shrapnel to fall like rain. Some nights you could hear it clattering on the roofs. Kids would go out the next morning collecting it. During air raids, it was dangerous to be out without a tin helmet.

St Helen's Cricket Ground today. This was a place of great fascination for kids during the war, who enjoyed watching the spectacular searchlight displays.

Alan also recalls,

> My Uncle John was a Royal Welsh Fusilier. He was home on embarkation leave and the whole family had gathered in my grandmother's house to wish him bon voyage. The siren went and we all trooped up the back garden into the Anderson Shelter. Brave Uncle John, something of a joker, insisted on standing outside. The Jerry bombs didn't frighten him. Suddenly a loud blast blew him in. 'Christ! That was near'. I can still hear my Auntie Rosa saying, 'You daft ha'porth, John, that wasn't a bomb, that was the ack-ack gun'. It was firing from behind our house.

Brian Owen recollects,

> At St Helen's Cricket Ground (the cricket field), there was an anti-aircraft battery complete with searchlights, and later in the war there was an anti-aircraft rocket site on the golf course at Ashleigh Road. Their practice firing was a great firework display.

INVASION PREPARATIONS

As a defence strategy against invasion by German forces, 'pill boxes' (fortified concrete bunkers) were built at several points along the Swansea beach at the sea wall, in the shadow of the 'big bridge' at the Slip and beyond 'the arch' at the end of Brynmill Lane. At Blackpill (mid-way around Swansea Bay), which the authorities considered the most likely landing site for an invasion force, great square concrete blocks were positioned to impede the progress of tanks. At the entrance to Clyne Valley, there were more 'pill boxes'.

On the beach below the high water mark, a large number of metal posts were embedded in the sand. These were old railway rails cut to size, set in a 'boulder' of concrete and secured by burying the 'boulder footing' in the sand. These were placed at an angle pointing out to sea. Set roughly 25 to 30 feet apart, they covered the large area between the low and high tide marks along the length of the beach from the docks to Blackpill. At high tide – the most likely time of any planned invasion – these posts were submerged and posed a potential hazard to landing craft.

Clearly, at this point in time, the authorities thought invasion was a distinct possibility but many pondered the effectiveness of these defences in impeding the progress of a determined enemy force. Some anti-invasion preparations posed deadly hazards for adventure-seeking kids – like the Caswell Bay minefield.

Brian Owen recalls,

> At Caswell, the narrow entrance to the bay at the end of the valley was a minefield, laid in preparation for a much anticipated German seaborne invasion. I recall talk of a child being killed there. Lots of kids threw stones over the barbed wire to see if the minefield was real. A narrow path to the side allowed access to the beach.

3

AIR-RAID SHELTERS

THOSE ANDERSON SHELTERS

The Anderson Shelter was a combination of well-intentioned optimism and poor design. Its potential in providing bomb protection for families was often brought into question. Sometimes, in reality, it was a miserable failure – though it must be said the Anderson Shelter did save many lives. However, since their designers took no account of waterproofing during wet weather, they filled with several inches of water, which made them damp and cold. Leaving a warm bed in winter for the miserable protection of a flooded Anderson shelter wasn't an easy decision, despite the danger. Often, Andersons were abandoned for alternative bomb protection arrangements within the house – these were at least warmer and drier. People like Swansea taxi driver Harry Stratton openly criticised the Anderson Shelter, and campaigned for better bomb protection. People like Len Owen (the author's father) took heed of this criticism and built his own indoor shelter.

Sylvia Loveridge, in her wartime memories of the Sandfields, preferred her Anderson Shelter to the communal shelter in the street. Bernard Evans and his family, in Waun Wen, found great protection in their Anderson, with a little help from a conveniently placed steel hoarding. Brian Owen, Len's son, hated theirs.

Sylvia Loveridge remembers her Anderson Shelter.

I was four-and-a-half years old when war was declared, but I remember well the air-raid shelter in our back garden. It was called an Anderson Shelter. My dad erected it and placed lots of soil on top and planted marigolds as camouflage. He hoped that the German bombers would think it was a garden.

The shelter was used a lot. Dad and Mam would take brother Raymond, sister June and myself from our beds out to the shelter when the siren sounded. Sometimes we would stay in the shelter all night. June and I were dressed in special suits. They were called siren suits and were basically all in one, from toe to head, with a flap at the back in case we had to go to the loo! They were similar to an outfit worn by Winston Churchill, the Prime Minister, in the war years.

We lived in Burrows Road, a cul-de-sac opposite St Helen's School in the Sandfields. In the middle of the road, a large red-brick shelter was built; it was mainly used by people who didn't have an Anderson shelter. We never liked it in the brick shelter as it was cold, damp and smelly. Young children always cried in there and were glad when it was morning. To make it more attractive to the little ones, Dad painted a lovely Union Jack on the front. The ugly shelter was an eyesore and was there for many years after the war, until it was eventually knocked down.

Mammy often made Welsh cakes on a grid on our open fire in the grate. It seemed we always had the sirens going when Mammy was cooking cakes. Often, when we were in the Anderson, she would run back to the house to turn the Welsh cakes over. I hated Mammy turning her cakes and was always glad when she came back safely.

While we were in the shelter, Dad was patrolling the school grounds and local streets fire-watching. He would come back to us every so often to see if we were all right. I used to hate it when we weren't all together.

Bernard Evans recalls how their Anderson shelter saved his family.

In late 1940, I was a six-year-old living in the Waun Wen area of Swansea. The area was already a target for German bombers because of the proximity to the Cwmfelin Steelworks. On the night in question, on hearing the air-raid warning, along with my parents and eight-year-old sister, I made my way to the Anderson Shelter in the back garden. My father had acquired a large steel advertising hoarding for 'Lyons Tea' and this was always placed at an angle across the entrance to the shelter, which faced the house. The hoarding was anchored with some sandbags and earth.

After what seemed like a short time, we heard aircraft approaching followed by some bangs. Suddenly there was an almighty bang very close and I can clearly remember hearing pieces of metal hitting the hoarding in front of our shelter. We were so terrified that our parents decided we should stay in the shelter even though everything had by then gone very quiet.

Eventually we heard a voice outside and my older brother, who had stayed the night with my aunt, appeared asking if we were alright. We slowly emerged from the shelter, and I can clearly remember seeing that where our house had been there was only a large gap in the terrace of houses. On the walls that were standing could be seen what had been fireplaces in the bedrooms. I recall my father saying 'My God! The house has gone!'

At this time we had no luxuries such as fridges and my mother kept her butter cool in a bowl of water on the kitchen floor. Her first words on seeing the devastation were 'and I put a new half pound of butter in the bowl last night!'

I still occasionally walk through Baptist Well Street and look at the two houses that replaced those that were bombed, and my thoughts go back to that night in 1940.

Brian Owen recalls,

The Anderson Shelter in our back yard was a disaster. It flooded every time it rained. At best it was always damp but, more often than not, the water in there was knee deep. It wasn't a healthy place and we hated it, but there were nights when it was the safest place to be. However, at the sound of the all-clear we couldn't get out of there fast enough.

Dad was a friend of Harry Stratton, who campaigned for shelters with more protection than the Anderson offered. Given the state of our shelter, and no doubt persuaded by Harry's arguments, Dad decided to build his own shelter inside the house. His shelter would be drier, healthier and would offer better protection. Through his work he was able to get hold of steel framework and corrugated sheets. He built our new shelter in the front room and we slept in it for some time. Everybody came to see our indoor shelter.

STREET SHELTERS
Arthur Colburn recalls,

By early 1941, my parents were getting organised for our visits to the street shelter. We took pillows, blankets, lamps, candles, small amounts of food and drink and every night, the Blitz-bag. This was a small case that contained jewellery, money, important documents like birth and death certificates, driving licences, ration books and so on. It was dark and damp down there, but at least the smell of fresh cement was starting to wear off.

The ladies sorted out the seating arrangements once they had got over the initial shock of having bombs dropped on them. Whoever sat nearest the door of the shelter listened for the all-clear. About forty or fifty of us would use this street shelter.

On 12 February, things got very bad. From where we were sitting inside the shelter, we could hear the explosions and when the all-clear sounded, we came out to find that Corporation Road on the other side of the river, had been severely hit. Seven people had been killed. A friend of mine, Owen Reynolds, who lived in that area at the time, told me some interesting facts about this particular raid.

Some of the victims in the street were children who had been evacuated to Port Talbot from various parts of the country, in the mistaken belief that it would be safer. This made the deaths even more tragic. A torpedo bomb landed in Leslie Street and other bombs landed in Wellington Place. Owen and his family, together with their neighbours, were taken to the Constitutional Club in Station Road and to the Masonic Hall in Forge Road. While this was going on, unexploded bombs were being dealt with by the bomb disposal unit. People in our town of Port Talbot, were finally coming to terms with what war was really about. Much worse was to follow just seven days later.

Bernard Evans recalls doubts about Anderson Shelters.

After the destruction of our home in Waun Wen, we were rehoused by the council in Mayhill where we fairly soon had incendiary bombs dropped in our garden. We again had an Anderson shelter in the garden, but by this time I think my parents had lost confidence in them. By now, my father had joined the Home Guard and I recall one occasion he took me to see the gun site where he was based at Ashleigh Road. I don't think, as a seven year old, I appreciated the significance of all the guns and the activity. It was just an exciting trip with my dad.

The air raids continued with only my mother to look after my sister and I. We no longer used the Anderson shelter in the garden, and as soon as the air-raid warning had sounded my mother would gather up my sister and I and hurry us from Mayhill down Waun Wen Road to a large communal air-raid shelter under St Joseph's School in Llangyfelach Street. This was quite a distance. I didn't appreciate the distance at the time, nor the fact that my mother's parent's home was immediately opposite the shelter.

As an adult I now think that my mother felt safer in the shelter near her family home and in the company of family and friends – even though we had to travel more than a mile to get there.

Even though I was only a child aged between six and ten during the war, I can clearly recall the close camaraderie that existed between people, and the trouble they would go to help one another. Something that, unfortunately, you don't find in communities today.

4

HOME AWAY FROM HOME: EVACUEES AND REFUGEES

The feeling that Swansea was a comparatively safe home front was quickly dispelled with the first bombing raids that occurred soon after the Fall of France. Many were alarmed by the fact that Swansea was now well within the range of enemy bombers, and some families lost no time in making arrangements for their children to be evacuated to the safety of the countryside. This activity was stepped up as the raids became more frequent and heavy. With mounting casualties and loss of life, as the town centre descended into a shambles of smoldering rubble, many sought to evacuate their entire families to safer places. This, however, ultimately turned into a desperate exercise, as there was little or no accommodation available within a 20 mile radius of the town.

As the Luftwaffe intensified its bombing raids, terror overtook and destabilized the town's population. Driven by the ferocity of the Three Night Blitz, many took to the open road on foot to escape the destruction. The chaos and devastation left no room for planned evacuation, people simply became refugees fleeing for their lives. Some were so desperate they sought the safety of the dark and wintry Gower countryside. People living close to the town centre joined the throng of refugees heading towards Sketty, and beyond, carrying their children, treasured possessions and any food and bedding they needed to survive the winter night.

Brian Owen, then six and a half, remembers a cold night and a long walk.

> The town was in flames and bombs were raining down. Carrying my younger brother, my mother, my father and I walked all the way to Gorseinon where we were taken in by friends. It was a cold night and the walk was long and tiring.

Much has been written about children who were evacuees. This is largely due to the fact that there was a great deal of publicity given to the government's initiative to evacuate children from the major cities such as London. Consequently, it is an area of children's wartime experience that is reasonably well-documented. Children who were evacuees were newsworthy; they received much media attention and were positively encouraged to tell their stories. The harrowing war experiences of children in general, however, went largely unrecorded. Apart from mostly posed photographs depicting children playing in blitz rubble – often for journalistic effect – the frontline fears and suffering of kids in the Second World War was, to a significant extent, deftly marginalized by officials. In all wars, or so it would seem, the suffering of children is a no-go area. Officialdom always seems forced by circumstance to downplay the suffering of kids in its efforts to tread a fine line between censorship and manipulative morale-boosting propaganda. The public record is scant on the experiences of children caught up in terrifying bombing raids, devastating fires, nerve-racking defensive anti-aircraft fire and the general terror and unsettling social upheaval that war brought to the doorsteps of their homes. These children simply had no public voice – a fact that might have suited the authorities at the time in their efforts to keep morale high, but now presents a serious omission in terms of information on the suffering of an important element of our community in times of war.

It would seem, even as evacuees, children were subjected to suffering. While being afforded 'safe' refuge in their new homes, some were treated badly and shamefully exploited. Vulnerable and already badly traumatized by separation, evacuee children were sometimes put at risk, and while wartime authorities did the best they could under extremely difficult conditions, not all evacuees enjoyed the comfort and security of a good home away from home.

John, Maureen and Peggy were three Swansea kids who went to good homes as evacuees but have greatly differing feelings about the experience.

Peggy's Story

Peggy O'Neil Davies gives us a glimpse of life as an evacuee. Her account is laced with sensitivity. The tag 'evacuee' undoubtedly set kids apart, but Peggy's experience was a positive one. Although tinged with an understated heartache that came from attachments that were formed, everything turned out well in the end. 'A lot of people were killed ... including friends. My mother and father decided that I should be evacuated.'

I was nearly ten years of age when the Second World War was declared and really didn't think it would make any difference to me. It was the grown ups that were talking about it but they didn't think it would change things much or last long. However, life changed dramatically for us children.

The bombing of Swansea became heavier and more frequent. After three nights in a row, a lot of houses were bombed and a lot of people were killed, including friends of mine and of my parents. My mother and father decided that I should be evacuated. They didn't talk to me about it, I was just told I was going. My mother came with me to see me settled and to see where I was going to live. We went by train to the nearest town, then up the valley by bus. I had always lived in a town and here I was going through these mountains and green fields.

The house I went to stay at had two children, a boy and a girl. Their mother did her best to make me feel welcome before my mother left me with these strangers. However, they were so good I really didn't feel homesick.'

Peggy continues,

At the beginning we were 'the evacuees', but soon we were accepted in the village and in the school (in the next village) to which we had to walk every day.

At first, the boy and girl I lived with were teased at having this 'evacuee' with them. To overcome this, parties and different things were organized for all evacuees who came from the various big cities. We were special and the villagers were determined to make us welcome. When evacuee parties were organised, the host children were always invited too. This went some way to making evacuees important children among their peers.

After living through the bombing of Swansea, life in the country was lovely. Climbing mountains, fruit picking, paddling in a little river that was called the brook – and no sirens!

When it came to sitting the entrance exam for a grammar school, the evacuees had to sit it together as they would have to go to a grammar school further down the valley. Sitting this exam was a big milestone. The 'Auntie' I lived with packed a special lunch as I had to be away all day and we had our own bus to take us and bring us back.

I was very lucky. I was in a good house, loved and treated as their own and my parents were able to visit me once a month. A lot of evacuees didn't see their parents at all while they were away. My mother sent me a parcel every week that included three of everything, so the children of the house looked forward to my parcel every Saturday. They were most upset when it didn't arrive on time at week's end.

I had been away one and a quarter years when I went home for a school holiday – my mother asked me if I'd like to come home. I was delighted, but my 'Auntie' had told my parents I didn't want to go back to Swansea (she knew she had come to love me and didn't want me to go home), so my mother decided at the end of the term I would no longer be an evacuee.

I was glad to be home but I had very happy memories of my time as an evacuee. I had enjoyed it and still keep in touch with my second family.

MAUREEN'S STORY

Maureen Lewis was also an evacuee, but Maureen's story focuses on the circumstances leading up to her flight to the comparative safety of Ponthenri, and the home of Mrs Quick. Her account gives us a graphic insight into the impact of war on a little girl, and the deep and lasting sense of 'loss' of the joys of childhood that was the legacy of her war.

I can hear it now, the siren. A wailing sound from a low note to a terrifying shrill crescendo. The warning. An air raid was about to start. The low throbbing sound of engines, then a whistle, breathtaking silence, an explosion. The night sky aflame.

My mother scooped my two brothers and I into her arms and raced us through the passageway of the house and into the cupboard under the staircase. My sobs made my shoulders shake. I didn't know what was happening, I was only four or five years old, I was very, very frightened.

Our home was in the centre of the seaport town of Swansea. A target for the enemy who wanted to destroy our ships and us into the bargain. Who could hate us so much, I didn't understand.

We were huddled together under the stairs, my mother mumbled words of prayer, begging God for our redemption. Then the siren again, but this time, descending in sound announcing that the enemy had gone away – at least for the time being. We crawled from the cupboard, into the pitch darkness of the house. All the windows were covered with blackout blinds. Not a chink of light was to be seen from outside that may give direction to the enemy in the skies above.

Maureen recollects,

I think that some expressions became an integral part of our language at the time. Words like 'bombed buildings', 'ration books', 'clothes coupons', 'national dried milk' – these were everyday expressions that belonged to this era of shortages brought about by war.

I remember Thursdays. This was the day that my mother had been to Lovell's sweet shop, next to the Albert Hall cinema. She knew Mr Lovell personally, so, her sweet ration coupons became elastic, but only because he was sympathetic with her having three children to treat! Dora, his assistant, would measure out into the bright scoop of the weighing scales, 2 ounces of this and that, until the required amount, measured by brass weights placed on the opposite side of the weighing scale scoop, was reached. Plus 1 or 2 ounces extra. The ration book was handed over, the coupons removed and the sweets were poured into cone-shaped paper bags, twirled around to a close at the top and handed over. The sweets were all tipped out onto a plate at home, and while reciting 'one for you' and 'one for you' and 'one for you', my mother shared out the boiled peardrops and humbugs. Ooh, I loved Thursdays.

From my vague memory, our lives at that time seemed to be ruled by the sound of the siren. The decision was made. My mother, her sister, my cousin, my two brothers and I were to flee into the country to apparent safety. The cupboard under the stairs had outlived its usefulness, the odds, seemingly, were too high. My father was home on leave from his unit – the RASC – and was there to wave us off as we left by car.

We journeyed through the town where heartbreaking sights met us. So much damage had been done, so many bombed buildings. Of the market hall, where my mother and aunt had a glass and china stall, only a shell remained. The fine old building, once covered by a glass roof, destroyed. Who would hate us so much to do this? I cried and cried because I didn't understand.

We continued our journey, which by today's reckoning is a stone's throw from Swansea, but then Ponthenri was in the back of beyond. Mrs Quick met us at the door of her home. I didn't know who this woman was who had opened her house up and welcomed a family who had run away from possible death. Did my mother know her, or my aunt? Was her name on a list of volunteers? I don't know. I didn't like it there. I didn't understand.

Maureen continues,

With memories fading fast as age overwhelms thoughts of those days so long ago, still there are lucid thoughts of the horror, the fear. Locked in a corner of my mind are feelings that cannot be faced even now. War lost for me the joys of my childhood. When, between the ages of four and ten, when life should have been filled with happiness, it was full of fear. Those years were taken from me by the futility of armed combat, men waging war against each other to prove superiority. Even the love of my parents could not redeem my childhood. There were many like me.

Schooldays saw us practising how to put on a gas mask. Protection from the evil of those who would completely destroy the lives of children. I didn't understand.

As I relate these memories, albeit vague, anger swells within me that the thoughts of my childhood are clouded in remembrances of the sound of bombs, flames leaping high into the night sky, my mother's mumbled prayers. Fear, which I did not understand. A part of my life was taken away from me and will never be retrieved.

JOHN'S STORY

John Lewis, like Peggy O'Neil Davies, was a lone evacuee. As a frightened and apprehensive six- or seven-year-old, John met Mrs Ebsworth who provided John with a loving home away from home.

John's experience as an evacuee is related by his wife, Maureen.

John, my husband of forty-three years, at the age of six or seven, was a bona fide evacuee. While I was lucky enough to be surrounded by my loving family while in exile, he was alone.

The decision to send one's children into the unknown must have been horrendous for the parents of that time. John had a brother two years his junior, his mother thought him too young to be sent away from home. She, meanwhile, in that winter of 1940, was heavily pregnant with child number three. In their front room was a metal table under which they would clamber when the dreaded sound of the siren started.

John's father, home on leave from the Royal Navy, and an uncle, put a wardrobe in the bay of the window to muffle the sounds of the explosions. That night, in November 1940, at the start of the air raid, under that very table, John's mother went into a very speedy labour and produced a third son. There were tears of joy and tears of fear as the throbbing sound of enemy aircraft passed overhead, en route to the docks where they dropped their lethal cargo.

John wore a label on his coat that clearly stated his name. He was taken by his mother to the local school. There were a number of other children gathered there, all labelled in the same way. They were shepherded onto a bus. Small faces, tears running down their cheeks, waving pathetically to their parents who knew that they might never see their children again. The bus travelled some 20 miles to a school in Llangennech, Carmarthenshire. Again a feat of transportation in those days.

They were taken into a classroom where other children were already sitting on the floor. They followed suit.

John was apprehensive and frightened as he looked around the room. Women, all strangers, were gathered there and one by one they chose a child to take home with them for the duration of the conflict. The children were handed over to supposed saviours. People who would care for them, or maybe not, but nevertheless, people who had volunteered to 'take' and house a child. Then, John spotted the most ugly woman he had ever seen. She must surely have been a witch. He quickly hid under the teacher's desk and listened to the movements hoping that the witch would take another child, any other child.

Then, he heard a woman's voice bemoaning the fact that there were no children left, she had wanted a boy to look after. He crawled out from his hiding place declaring that he was a boy, to face a lady who was to be his mother, his protector, his guardian for the following two years. He knew when he looked at her that he would like this Mrs Ebsworth. Though no substitute for his mother, this lady took this little boy, a complete stranger, and provided him with a loving home. John still thinks fondly of this lady.

These three accounts give us small but significant insights into childhood, fractured by war. They serve to remind us how harsh wartime conditions impacted on young lives. All children caught up in war are vulnerable. Trauma was inevitable when young children were dislodged from their homes, separated from the parents and forced, by circumstances, to trust unknown people in strange surroundings that they were to call 'home'. Disruptive and disturbing though evacuation was, those kids who found good homes might well be regarded as 'the lucky ones'.

It should be said that a great deal of the evacuee experience wasn't heartache and tragedy. For many kids it was a great adventure. It opened up new beginnings in exciting surroundings, and the chance to make new and enduring friendships, but evacuation also had its dark side. Some kids suffered devastating hardship: bad homes; unloving and exploitative guardians; exposure to danger. For some, their trauma was compounded by loss. Some never saw their mothers and fathers again, losing both parents to a combination of the Blitz and death on active service.

5

THE LONE RAIDER:
ONE OF HERMANN GOERING'S PIRATES

The Fall of France on 14 June 1940 put Swansea on the road to destruction and misery. While this momentous event generated much talk of a German invasion, and stimulated the Authorities into hastily implementing some rudimentary anti-invasion strategies, the consequences of the capitulation of the French seemed remote to the majority of the population. Although the prospect of air attacks and seaboard landings filled everyone with foreboding, it was the general, if erroneous, opinion of many that Swansea would remain a relatively safe home front and that, with luck, the Phoney War conditions (which, in fact, ended a month earlier) would continue for 'the duration'.

The Phoney War was that period between 3 September 1939 and 10 May 1940. It commenced with the declaration of war and ended when the German Army marched into the Low Countries.

During this period, there was lull in hostilities between Britain and Germany. RAF and the Luftwaffe bombers refrained from making deliberate attacks on each others towns and cities. It was this lull in the West that was to give people a false sense of security. Their country was at war, but apart from wartime restrictions nothing seemed to happen. Hence the period was referred to as the Phoney War.

People felt complacent and the tag 'Phoney War' further added to this complacency. In the absence of conflict between Germany and Britain, the British population felt that their government, with its war of words, had been over-reactive and over-cautious. This feeling continued in Swansea even after the Fall of France – a fact that was to make the first enemy attack on the town, with its 'It couldn't happen to us' attitude, more psychologically damaging.

With the subjugation of France, the picture was to change dramatically. Targets on the western side of Britain fell within the Luftwaffe's range. Bomber units of Luftflotte 3 moved to capture French airfields west of the River Seine, and Swansea was in for a rough time, at the mercy of fully loaded bombers.

However, for kids, and anyone else who used Swansea Beach for recreation at this time, the extent of the anti-invasion measures induced a chill of fear. Rumour spread far and wide rapidly. Swansea Bay was the likely site of a German invasion. This notion was given further credence when public access to the beach was prohibited. Rumour

Dramatic reconstruction of one of Herman Goering's Lone Raider Pirates over Swansea Bay.

had it that the entire beach had been covered in oil, which would be ignited in the event of troop landings.

Spectacular stuff! However, anti-invasion activity proved more effective in putting Swansea people 'off their guard' as regards possible air raids, than any other single factor. This feverish activity, on the part of the authorities, had the population more focused on a seaboard invasion than on air attack. Things, however, were about to change.

Thirteen days after the Fall of France, in the early hours of a Wednesday morning while the town slept, and totally without warning, Swansea experienced its first air attack. It was considered a minor raid, with only six high explosive bombs dropped in the vicinity of Kilvey Hill and Danygraig Road (four of which failed to explode), and no casualties and only minor damage to property. The attack brought home to the people of Swansea the extent of their vulnerability. They were now within reach of the Luftwaffe – a fact that struck fear into young and old.

Two days later, in the early hours of the morning, and again without warning, there was another minor air raid. This time the attack was on an industrial target in Morriston, the Upper Forest and Worcester Tinplate Works. Though only four bombs were dropped, and again without casualties, everybody was inclined to think that air raids would only occur under the cover of darkness. In this they were greatly mistaken.

After a respite of eleven days, there was a daylight attack on Swansea docks. This caused extensive damage to sheds and workshops. Twenty-six people were injured and thirteen dockers were killed.

Harry Stratton recalls that the raid took place with captured planes.

> It was a daylight raid in which the Germans used captured French planes and took
> everyone by surprise. The raid was on the Docks, and E Shed on the Mole at the top
> of the King's Dock, and the nearby canteen were hit. Thirteen dockers were killed.
>
> (*To Anti-Fascism by Taxi,* Harry Stratton, Alun Books, South Wales, UK)

Brian Owen, then six years old, also remembers that first daylight raid.

> I was on the beach playing with some other kids from our street. There was a daylight
> raid. The docks were bombed. Dockers were machine-gunned and killed.

The attack at 10.20 a.m. came without warning. It was brief and had a devastating
effect on everyone. Gone was the relative quiet of the home front. The enemy was now
as close and as deadly as in any frontline situation.

Daylight raids caused serious concern for everyone all over the country. Often
these raids were carried out with lightning speed by lone German fighter bombers.
These lone raiders struck fear into all who saw them. Brian Owen vividly recalls
a very close and frightening encounter with one of these German pirate raiders in
broad daylight.

PIRATE ATTACKS

Early in the war, Hermann Goering had issued an edict. If weather conditions over
Britain didn't favour large-scale bombing operations, then heavily armed individual
fighter bombers would engage in surprise daylight attacks on selected targets.

These 'hit-and-run' attacks were carried out by experienced and highly-skilled
aircrews in a daredevil spirit. Under the protection of poor weather conditions,
which helped prevent interception by RAF fighters, they flew below the cloud cover,
skimming rooftops at an altitude of no more than thirty metres. The attacks were swift
and deadly – the strategy was to damage and demoralise.

These missions were referred to, by Luftwaffe aircrews as *Pirateneinsatz,* or Pirate
Attacks. Pirate Attacks were so fast and unpredictable they made successful interception
by RAF fighters extremely difficult.

In addition to the devastation that these 'lone raiders' could inflict on specific
targets they also had a powerful psychological effect. The idea of unchallenged, bomb-
carrying enemy aircraft, flying extremely low over populated areas, had a profound
demoralising effect on the population.

Brian recollects,

> One day I was on the corner of Gorse Lane and St Helen's Avenue, outside the Brockley
> Café. Suddenly, a low flying Heinkel passed over the 'Cricketers'. I was flattened by
> a soldier who was garrisoned in the cricket field and happened to be passing by. The

This photographic reconstruction of the roof-skimming Heinkel fighter bomber at the very spot in Gorse Lane where Brian Owen saw and heard the terrifying noise of one of these lone raiders mirrors Brian's retelling of the incident.

noise, the unexpected close-up view of this terrifying war machine, and the soldier's reflex action were all a bit frightening – but it was also very exciting. I could clearly see the pilot and the gunners. Suddenly the enemy and their threat became very real. I never imagined seeing Germans at such close quarters.

Typical of a pirate raider, the lone low-flying Heinkel skimmed the rooftops, flying just 30 metres above the ground. Flying away from the centre of the town, below the level of Terrace Road, the highly-skilled pilot flew the narrow corridor between the tower of the Civic Centre (with its protective barrage balloon and cables) and the base of the Uplands and Brynmill Hill, along the line of King Edwards Road.

Maintaining this extremely low, daredevil altitude, the Heinkel flew directly over the Cricketer's Hotel and the cricket field turning gradually to follow the shoreline of the bay. Passing over two ships beached at West Cross and dropping 'something' in their vicinity, the plane barely cleared the cliff at Dickslade in Mumbles before heading off down the Bristol Channel to its base in France.

The two ships beached at West Cross were, in all likelihood, the Blue Funnel steamer *Protesilaus*, from the Far East, and the Motor Tanker *Seminole*.

Both these ships were beached at West Cross after being the victims of magnetic mines in the Bristol Channel. Mined ships were often beached so that they could be salvaged later or broken up for valuable scrap.

There doesn't appear to be any record of bombing of Swansea by this aircraft. It might well have been that this raider had been disrupted in its attack on another target, possibly Bristol, where it might have been driven off by RAF fighters and forced to make its escape by hugging the Welsh coast, possibly in search of other targets. After flying over Swansea and heading for the Bristol Channel and his home base in France, the pilot of the Heinkel raider might have just happened upon these beached ships and, on the spur of the moment, decided to further damage them (since they were directly in his flight path) by unloading any remaining bombs. It is not clear whether these bombs exploded, or if indeed they were bombs that were dropped.

The Heinkel, seen at such close quarters, was an awesome war machine. The roar of its engines was menacing. Independently, two children and a man with a baby in a pram witnessed this low flying 'pirate'. Clifford Davies, the baker from Nelson Street Bakery, was out walking with his baby daughter, Maureen, in a pram. They were between the Hospital Square and the Brangwyn Hall, when the plane roared by – well below the line of houses on Terrace Road. Brian Owen was directly under its flight path.

Another youngster, Alan Davies, who lived in Mumbles, was standing at Dickslade that morning. Years later he and Brian became friends. On hearing Brian's story, Alan related how he saw the same Heinkel, flying very low, coming across the bay towards him. Directly between Alan and the on-coming plane were two ships that had been beached at West Cross. Alan related how he saw what looked like two 'bombs' being dropped as the plane passed over the ships before it flew directly overhead barely clearing the cliff.

The noise and sight of these death-delivering war machines, in daylight, just above the rooftops, was terrifying. The idea that they could penetrate RAF air defenses, at will, was unsettling. In spite of the fact that there were comparatively few of these 'pirate' attacks in the Swansea area, their lethal potential and audacity put many 'on edge'. Without an air-raid warning and the opportunity to take shelter, they made people feel extremely vulnerable.

6

THE THREE NIGHT BLITZ

The following narrative is based on fragmented recollections and facts from a variety of sources. It is not intended to be an accurate historical account but rather a graphic reconstruction to serve as a setting for people's childhood recollections. These childhood memories give us glimpses of the worst of the bombing. Some are from children who viewed the destruction of Swansea from a distance while others are from kids caught up in its midst. Collectively, they provide us with a detailed image of children's experience of frontline war.

ILL MET BY MOONLIGHT

Shortly after dark on 19 February 1941, Swansea, and its surrounding hills, were dusted with a light covering of snow. The snow showers soon passed, and with a clearing sky the usual pitch-blackness of the blacked-out town on a winter's night was banished by unexpectedly bright moonlight. Bathed in soft blue-grey light, the town presented an atmosphere of peace and tranquility, a tranquility that belied the death and mayhem that lay in the night ahead.

The unusually light night saw quite a few people on the streets: couples taking the night air; people going to the cinema; friends visiting friends; ARP wardens on night patrol; a lone cyclist braving the slippery road on their way home from work; a group of kids excited by the snow, but bemoaning the lightness of the fall; a man walking his dog; a priest from St David's church in Rutland Street on his way to share an evening meal with an Italian family, all unsuspecting of the danger heading their way.

At about 7.30 p.m., just after younger kids would have been put to bed, the mournful wail of the air-raid sirens shattered the peace and sent everyone scuttling for shelter. Parents snatched children from their beds and sleepy-eyed kids were made comfortable in candle-lit cupboards under the stairs and in backyard air-raid shelters. Pets were called to join them – dogs heeding the call while cats resolutely sat perched on snow-dusted moonlit walls savouring the night. Small children gradually awoke and picked up on an all-pervading sense of anticipation mixed with fear. The waiting was interminable as people in their shelters everywhere sat quietly listening for the distant sound of the incoming aircraft.

Meanwhile, the German bombers droned their way up the Bristol Channel in formation. The aircrews of their pathfinders 'edgy' but excited. The brightness of the night not only made the aircraft conspicuous, but would also help them find their target. Their low-flying approach up the Channel was so low and so close to the Gower coast that people there reported being able to see the German markings.

Keeping well clear of the anti-aircraft guns on Mumbles Head, the bombers began their climb to altitude. It seems likely that they continued their climb, while crossing the coast in the Port Talbot area. Somewhere to the north-east of Neath, they banked left to pick up the course of the river in the Vale of Neath, which they then followed towards the sea. Observed flying high over Neath, in formations of three, they were then seen to bank to the right at the estuary to make their bombing run on Swansea.

The pathfinders, who readily found their mark, dropped their flares to the seaward of the town – the bright flares illuminating the target for following bombers carrying thousands of incendiary bombs and payloads of high explosives.

About 56,000 incendiary bombs were dropped on Swansea during the Three Night Blitz.

THE GHOST TRAIN

David Davies provides us with details of interruptions to a night's entertainment that were typical of the time. His telling of his childhood experience underscores the fact that, while enjoying public entertainment, warnings of danger often went largely unheeded – until things got seriously dangerous and people literally fled for their lives.

David recalls,

> On a clear night in 1941, my uncle Mr Gwilym Evans was producing the play *The Ghost Train* at the Welfare Hall Fforestfach, Swansea. The play was well into the first act, when, to our surprise, Uncle Gwilym appeared on the stage. He delivered what had become a standard warning of an air raid over Swansea. It went the usual way: 'Ladies and Gentlemen, we have been informed by the police that an air-raid warning has been sounded and it is our duty to inform you of this fact. We shall be carrying on with the play but those of you who wish to leave should do so now.'

David continues,

> At this point, a few people left, but not many. As ten-year-olds, my two friends and I were far too brave to be frightened by warnings like that. We had seen them too often, they flashed up on the screens of local cinemas and usually for nothing in the end. So the play continued. The effects were excellent. I remember the windows of the lighted train becoming visible through the windows of the railway station, and the sounds of the train drawing to a halt. Just as the play was becoming suitably creepy, my uncle appeared on the stage again. This was halfway through the second act. This time the warning was more urgent. 'We have to tell you, Ladies and Gentlemen, that

the police have now ordered us to stop the play and to allow you to go home. Please do so quietly'.

At this, my two friends and I looked at each other, shrugged our shoulders and left the Welfare Hall and started towards our homes. By the time we were halfway along Armine Road, which ran past our old school (Gendros School), we had the experience of seeing an orange glow rising above Townhill. We were also starting to hear the whine of bombs but could not see any explosions – they were over the hill towards the town and docks. I started to think, with some pleasure, of the prospects of no school the following day when another shrill whine of bombs came out of the sky.

This time, several incendiary bombs exploded down part of Armine Road and we flattened ourselves against the walls of the houses opposite the school, just as we had seen them do in the films of the period. We paused on the corner of King's Head Road and Armine Road, where a small group were saying goodnight before heading off in different directions. We ran a few yards towards Carmarthen Road, heard another loud scream of bombs and a stick of incendiaries straddled King's Head Road, not many yards from the corner we had just turned. By then, our roles as war heroes were to wearing a little thin. The next stick of bombs was too close for comfort.

There were burning incendiaries everywhere, one of which was being extinguished by Glan Jenkins, an air-raid warden and our Sunday School teacher. I parted company with one friend who lived near Fforestfach Cross and turned left with the other. We ran home to the arms of our parents who had, of course, been frantic with worry. My own mother had had to be restrained by my grandparents, apparently, from coming to look for me. We spent the rest of that night under the stairs, listening to the frightening sounds of the high explosive bombs raining down on Swansea 3 miles away. That was the first night of the Three Night Blitz on Swansea.

THE TOWN ABLAZE

Eric Wydenbach lived with his family in the centre of Swansea. Although very young at the time, his recollections give us a dramatic sense of the fire storm that accompanied the destruction of the town centre.

During the whole of the Second World War, we lived in upper Plymouth Street in the centre of town. At the time of the worst period, the three night bombings, I was three years old – so obviously can't remember it, right? No, wrong! I have a number of fragmented and mixed-up memories, and one very clear one.

During the three nights (when most of the town centre was destroyed), my mother and I did not leave the house. She was afraid to go outside during the raids. We lived behind a shop (The Direct Coal Co.) and the police and ARP didn't know anyone was living there, otherwise they would have hauled us out to a shelter.

There was destruction 70 metres west of us; 50 metres north; 120 metres east (the market, etc.) and 30 metres to the south. My mother must have been terrified but I was too young to take it all in. My father was a fireman, so was missing for the whole period, busy digging bodies out of Mayhill I expect. Then, during a lull in the raid on the third night, Mr Chilcott, who lived opposite us (the grandfather, I believe, of Gareth, the England Rugby Union player) and who spent the period in the nearest community shelter, came looking for us. We then went with him to the shelter (though the all-clear went minutes later), him carrying me. As we got out into the street, a street littered with incendiary bombs, you could see that buildings behind the Chilcotts (where the lower Picton Arcade is) facing us, were burning. I have this abiding memory of wanting to know: 'Why, instead of flames, the air was full of sparks, as one gets from burning wood.' I distinctly remember asking the question but I don't remember anyone answering.

Soon afterwards, they delivered a Morrison Shelter to us (a reinforced steel table that you slept underneath) but, although there were lots more bombs to come, there was to be nothing like those three nights.

Big Boys Don't Cry

Graham Davies tells us of the night when his house was hit by a bomb – a night of terror that reduced him to tears.

Big boys don't cry. Well, I was one who did. I cried and I was ashamed. Now, it is difficult to imagine what it was actually like to be bombed. First you heard the awful wailing of the sirens, then the relentless drone of the German bombers, followed by the bombs whistling, screaming down. It was terrifying. I was eight years old and I cried.

We were a family of four living in St Helen's Crescent, directly opposite the Civic Centre – my mum and dad, and my brother aged twelve. In February 1941, the Luftwaffe bombed Swansea on three consecutive nights, the worst being the third night when incendiary bombs created enormous fires in the town centre. When the warning sirens sounded, Mum, my brother and I huddled under the oak table in the kitchen. Suddenly, there was a swoosh and an ominous thud. Within seconds smoke was seeping under the scullery door. We'd been hit. Our house was on fire. To say that my Mum went berserk would be unfair – she was in a frenzy of action. Grabbing a bucket of water she set about the fire, at the same time shrieking orders to my brother and me to get out. We were to go to the hotel on the corner, which was owned by my uncle.

Outside was a menacing fairyland. The Civic Centre greens were dotted with burning flares creating battlefield conditions. My brother grabbed my arm and we ran to the safety of the Civic Hotel cellar. Seemingly we were only there for minutes when my mum arrived having, unbelievably, extinguished the fire with help from some neighbours. She was breathless and indignant. She kept repeating that my dad was putting out other people's fires, while his own house was in danger.

Nobody slept that night. As we ate an early breakfast, reports of the damage came in. Mr Powell, a neighbour of ours, was in a miserable condition: dirty, dishevelled and tired. He was handed a mug of tea. He drooped in the chair and told his story. 'The old town was ablaze … they had run out of water … helplessly they had to watch the centre of Swansea … they had to watch the centre of Swansea being destroyed'. He wept. It was the first time that I had ever seen a man cry. I can see him now as he blubbered out his story.

I was no longer ashamed. I wasn't the only one who had cried that night.

WHISTLING BOMBS
Alfred John Whitby recalls a direct hit demolished a row of houses.

On one evening, Teilo Crescent in Mayhill took a direct hit, which demolished a row of houses. I cannot recall the number of fatalities, but I believe it was quite substantial.

Many a night the sirens would sound to warn us of an imminent air raid and we would all take to the shelters for protection. The sky would be lit up by the flares dropped from German bombers, prior to what we called the 'whistling bombs'.

Brian Owen recalls,

During one heavy raid, we could hear the bombs whistling as they fell towards us. It was a terrifying sound. We all braced ourselves thinking 'this is it'!

This particular night there were a number of people in the street outside our house on fire watch. When they heard the bombs coming, they ran into the house and dived into our shelter. It was a bit frightening with bodies piled on top of each other. The bombs landed in the street and a number of houses were hit – thankfully, not ours. When the danger had passed, and things went quiet again, someone commented, 'That was a close one – let's see if we can help the poor bastard down the Avenue.' There was a big cloud of dust and smoke in the street. The house opposite what used to be Hunt's Bakery had been badly damaged.

VIEW ACROSS THE BAY
The sight of Swansea burning during the Three Night Blitz etched itself into the minds of children of all ages. The very young Neil Gordon, who grew up in Mumbles, remembers being carried to a window to see the blazing spectacle. The significance of what he saw was lost on him, but older children, like Ken Gravelle in Aberavon, measured the gravity of what they saw by the remarks of their parents.

What **Ken Gravelle** saw:

'Put that light out' shouted the ARP warden, as he banged on one of the doors of the long street of terraced houses at the western side of Aberavon.

One of the residents had dared show a chink of light through the curtains. Our group of ten- and eleven-year-olds who lived in the street, thought this quite funny, as the winter nights were frequently lit up by the glare from the nearby Port Talbot blast furnaces as they were tapped for their molten steel. By this reddish-orange glow we were able to play for several minutes during the blackout hours.

But the February nights of 1941 were to bring us another light in the sky. It was towards the end of the month that we heard the distinctive throb of the German bomber planes overhead – we had quickly learned to differentiate the sound of 'theirs' and 'ours'. But we were not the target this time. The ack-ack guns in the woodlands behind Baglan Church opened fire, but their chances of scoring a hit were remote.

When the raids were over, I remember being taken by our parents to a raised piece of waste land at the end of the street. From here we could look across the moorlands (now heavily built on), across the bay to Swansea – 12 miles distance by road but only 2 to 3 miles across the water. Swansea was burning. We could see the huge orange dome in the skies above the town. The next morning, when we went again to our viewing place, it was to see the huge pall of smoke that lay over the stricken area.

At the time, we young lads did not fully appreciate the true significance of what had happened, but our elders were in no doubt of the appalling tragedy that we were witnessing. 'They'll pay for this' said my father, who had fought in the 1914–18 war, and pay they did, when later the 1,000 bomber raids attacked Germany. A dreadful price!

WE LIVED IN FEAR

Children not only had to cope with their own fear and anxiety, they also watched, helplessly, as the war took its terrible toll on their parents – some of whom had dangerous night jobs that kept them from knowing the fate of their families during air raids.

Joan Thomas recalls,

The winter of 1941 was the worst of the war for Swansea. Every night saw us getting up, putting on warm clothes over our pyjamas and trooping down to the Anderson Shelter in the garden. Armed with hot water bottles and blankets, we bedded down for the night. We emerged bleary-eyed into the cold morning to view the damage done.

My father was a railwayman working on Swansea Docks. Every other week he worked nights taking oil-freight trains to Llandarcy Oil Refinery. Coming home in the early mornings, he picked his way around bomb craters and rubble. He used to dread turning the corner to our street in Manselton, in case our house had been hit. Eventually, he had to stay at home, off work, his nerves shot to pieces and his head covered in patches of alopecia.

'SEEN OUR CRATER?'

Unable to take shelter because he was ill, **Roger Jones** stayed in bed during one air raid. His wife, Doreen, tells his story of a near miss.

My husband, Roger Jones, had a traumatic time. A bomb exploded in the drive of their house in Glanmor Road. All the family, except him, were sheltering in the basement. He remained in the upstairs front room, adjacent to the driveway, because at the time he was ill.

The blast went upwards and outwards, with little damage to the house except to the windows. It has kept the family in yarns to this day as they greeted visitors with the family saying, 'That's war. Seen our crater?'

THE SMELL OF THE BLITZ

The smell of dust, charred brick and smouldering timber filled the night air as firemen fought to control the fires that ravaged the town. These are the smells that most people associate with the height of the town's of destruction, smells that lingered long after the blitz was over. For many wartime kids, the smell of burning candles in dark musty places evokes nights of terror spent under stairs and in cold Anderson shelters.

Alan Hughes recalls other smells associated with vivid war memories.

On 13 February 1941, I celebrated my seventh birthday. My sister, Dee, was only eighteen months old. We lived in Caereithin, diagonally opposite the heavily camouflaged Ravenhill bus garage, nine doors from the first farmer's fields. My most vivid memories of the Three Night Blitz are of the smells.

It must have been night one of the big Blitz. The siren sounded and Mum quickly dressed my sister and I in the siren suits that she had made. (They were based on a pattern worn by Winston Churchill). She put a few precious valuables in her shopping bag and, carrying my sister, she took us to the communal shelter built under the cricket pitch in Ravenhill Park. My enduring memory of the shelter was the overpowering smell of body odour. I held my nose and tried to breathe through my mouth. The fetid smell was made worse by the noise of crying children. They were joined by my sister and I.

On the second night, my mother was determined not to go to the shelter. Again dressed in our siren suits, my sister in her pram and me sitting on it, we were wheeled down the narrow country road to Cadle Mill.

After the all-clear we returned home and on the way we sat on the bridge over the Lliw stream and looked back at the glowing sky over Swansea. Drifting over the hill towards us was the smell of the burning town, a smell that stayed in the town for many years after. Although she kept a brave face, I could feel my mother's anxiety. Dad was at a first-aid post somewhere in the town.

On the third night, we again went into the country, a mile further this time to Penllegaer. We ended up in the New Moon pub. Again it was the smell I recall, a mixture of beer and tobacco. Perhaps this was the reason that, later in life, I spent twenty-five years as a publican.

THE FOLLOWING TWO NIGHTS

Nightmarish and terrifying as the Blitz was, for some kids there were compensations the next day.

David Davies recalls,

During the following two nights, we became used to the drone-drone-drone of the German bombers, the harsh crack of the anti-aircraft shells and the sound of exploding bombs. There was the bonus of no school the following day, and an allowance for going in late on further days. There is no denying the fact that we were frightened.

The scene of desolation was once the centre of a thriving town. A busy business hub, which people enjoyed from far and wide. Shopping, socialising or just enjoying the bustle of a busy town, Swansea was considered a fine and interesting place to spend a carefree day.

It was a nightmarish time as there was little to cheer about in those days. Then there was the shrapnel. Boys hunted for, swapped and compared the pieces of shrapnel they had collected. It was a great game. There were dismal sights to see on the way to school in Swansea. Bombed out shops, pools of blood, the whole top floor of my new school, Dynevor, completely gutted.

Boys exchanged lurid stories, often embellished, of the horrors they had seen. 'I saw a man putting a head in a bin' was one such tale.

DARTS, CARDS AND A LUCKY ESCAPE
Joan Thomas recalls,

On the third night of the Blitz, we had been invited by our neighbours to await the familiar wail of the siren. We played cards and darts and then joined them under the stairs, which they had made into a comfortable shelter.

The sirens went. The bombs started raining down. Very close this time and we heard and felt a terrific thump. Soon after, there was a knock on the door by an ARP man who ordered us out of the house. We were taken to a nearby church hall where we were given hot drinks and blankets.

The next morning we found out that the terrific thump we had heard was an unexploded bomb. It had landed in our garden right behind our Anderson shelter and

One of the many peacetime reconstructions of the Castle Gardens, showing the extensive redevelopment of what was a vast open bomb site. On the left-hand side of this prime position are various shops and businesses, which replaced a hotel and a large department store in the years before 1941 bombing of the town centre.

had flattened it. The windows in our house were shattered and all the ceilings had collapsed. The mess was indescribable, but by a miracle we were all safe.

God was looking out for us that night. If we had been in that shelter, I would not be writing this now.

SNOWBALLS AND BLOOD RED SKIES
Arthur Colburn recalls,

During the evening of 19 February 1941, we had celebrated my father's forty-seventh birthday. Being non-drinkers, my mother had put on a wartime high tea of jelly, cakes and sandwiches. The occasion was interrupted by sirens. Everyone headed for the shelters, except my father who was a police motor-cyclist and on duty.

It soon became obvious that this was what the Germans had been building up to. The sky seemed to be blood red as the incendiary bombs rained down, starting many fires, on this the first night of the Swansea Blitz. As the awful details came through and the adults tried to hide their tears, we children, not fully realising what had happened, had snowball fights.

'ALL CLEAR'

There was both relief and anxiety after the all-clear had sounded. Apart from the 'good to be still alive' feeling of having survived the onslaught, and the chance to catch up on lost sleep, there was much fear and loathing of what people were going to find the next day. Everyone ventured out expecting the worst yet hoping for the best.

The morning after the Three Night Blitz was painful for everyone. The centre of town was in ruins, and there was no way of knowing whether or not that was the end of it. Everyone was tense and braced themselves for a fourth night of bombing, which didn't eventuate. Nerves were ragged and children were irritable. Shrapnel littered the streets and there were many unexploded incendiary bombs lying about – St Helen's Cricket Field was littered with them. Bomb craters and bombed houses were everywhere. The town's former shopping centre was a heap of smouldering rubble. There was stunned disbelief at the stories one heard – stories of near misses and death, of shelters filled with hundreds of dead people. Myth and fact became inseparable companions in second- and third-hand stories. Some children lost school chums and relatives. Fathers went missing in the mayhem.

Rebuilt, the rubble that was the heart of the old town of Swansea was totally redeveloped into the thriving city of today, showing little or no evidence of the Three Night Blitz.

Children became distressed over lost pets missing for days, and sometimes weeks, having taken off in fright at the sound of exploding bombs and ack-ack gunfire. Kids went about the streets and lanes looking for their pet cats and dogs. Saucers of food were left untouched as days of distressing loss went by, but often the animals returned home, thin and dishevelled but safe.

INSPECTING THE DAMAGE

Many kids showed a keen interest in inspecting bomb damage after every air raid.

Brian Owen recalls,

After a raid we would go for a walk to see the damage. Several houses in the Avenue (St Helen's Avenue) were burnt down by incendiary bombs. Houses on Rhyddings Park Road and in Northampton Lane were bombed. There were bomb craters along the front, and one outside the entrance to the Brangwyn Hall, probably caused by an unexploded bomb because there didn't appear to be any damage to the building. There was another bomb crater on the railway line by the Cenotaph. Some bombs also landed on the beach – there were two craters near the 'Big Pipe' close to Swansea Bay railway station (opposite the cricket field).

Graham Davies also recalls the bomb that fell outside the entrance to the Brangwyn Hall.

Rumours spread rapidly – a Townhill Street had been destroyed with heavy loss of life; there were unexploded bombs in Phillip's Parade and in St Helen's Road, leading to the evacuation of patients from Swansea General Hospital. One of our teachers, Ossie Davies, had become a hero, injuring himself in rescuing a boy; another bomb had hit the Castle Cinema. It was all vague and bewildering, but it was exciting too. Surprisingly, we were allowed out to meet our friends. Perhaps our parents were too exhausted to stop us. We had survived a dreadful night and we needed to get outside for fresh air.

John Alfred Whitby remembers,

When the all-clear siren sounded (normally in the early hours of the morning) we would try to continue our sleep until daybreak, and then we all would go out and about looking at the devastation caused by the previous night's raid. I remember after one particular raid, my cousin, Allan Penhorwood, and myself were told that our aunt's house in Gorse Avenue had been bombed, so we ventured down to have a look to see what we could salvage for her and her family, who were not present at the house on the night of its bombing. It was rather curious and baffling, for while the house was almost completely ruined, a clock on the mantlepiece in the parlour remained in perfect working condition, and a bottle, half full of milk, stood upright on the kitchen table, while all around was total devastation.

The Cenotaph on the Prom was always a draw for kids in the Second World War, who not only marvelled at the numbers who had died, but enjoyed the environs for games like 'off ground touch' on Saturday mornings. On memorial days, attended by uniformed servicemen bearing flags, kids felt the solemness of the occasion. (*Stu Phillips*)

7

TAKEN BY STEALTH & BY FORCE: A KID'S EYE-VIEW

Impressionable and ever observant, wartime children often witnessed events and made mental note of things that were apparently trivial and insignificant at the time. However, on recall, and with the benefit of hindsight, what they saw sometimes proved to be of some significance.

IN A CLEAR PATCH OF BLUE
Brian Owen remembers,

> It was a few days after the Three Night Blitz. I was standing in the middle of the road outside our house in St Helen's Avenue. I was scanning the sky, something I did instinctively after all the air raids. It was a fine day with a few wispy clouds. I didn't hear anything, but in a clear patch of blue I saw the white underbelly of a plane flying very high towards Porthcawl, so high I couldn't hear its engines. Although I only had a brief glimpse, I was sure it was a German plane. I ran in to tell Mam who was preparing dinner. I can't remember what she said, but she didn't seem unduly concerned by what I saw.

What Brian observed was, in all likelihood, a German reconnaissance aircraft (probably a Junkers JU 86P), with its white underbelly providing some degree of camouflage – taking photographs of the damage inflicted on the town. The timing of his observation (around midday), and the prevailing weather conditions, point to a Luftwaffe reconnaissance flight on 24 February 1941.

GERMAN RECONNAISSANCE FLIGHTS
In the summer of 1940, after the Fall of France, Reichsmarschall Goering ordered his reconnaissance units to photograph vast areas of Britain, in preparation for bombing raids and invasion. Over the period 1940/41, Luftwaffe aircraft, equipped with sophisticated photographing equipment, flew high over the towns of Wales, either

alone or in small groups, providing high quality photographic views of their intended targets. The resulting photographs of Swansea and the Swansea Bay area reveal some incredible detail.

Junkers aircraft, like the Junkers JU 86P, had been specially adapted with pressurized cockpits and high-performance diesel engines to fly at extremely high altitude (41,000 feet) – well beyond the reach of British air defence forces. These aircraft, stationed on the outskirts of Paris, carried out reconnaissance for German air force bombing units based in places like Vannes in North Western France, from which Swansea was bombed.

This was most likely a lone aircraft engaged in a post-air-raid survey to provide feedback on the damage inflicted by the Three Night Blitz. It would have been flying at extremely high altitude, beyond the reach of local air defences, which would have been in a state of readiness following the raids.

Photographs taken on 24 February 1940, and from earlier surveys, are published in *Eye of the Eagle: The Luftwaffe Aerial Photographs of Swansea* by Nigel A. Robins.

PRESS GANGS AND THE WAR EFFORT

Sometimes kids witnessed the darker, untold side of the war effort.

During wartime, the humour-laced cynicism of adults often served as a defensive mechanism against the harsher realities of those difficult times. This is reflected in my mother's perspective on the story that follows. Children, on the other hand, tended to be less sophisticated and more open – their telling of events nearer the raw truth.

Often, the insights of kids into the harsher aspects of life in wartime revealed the darker side of the so called 'war effort' – as in the following case related by Brian Owen.

> I often heard my mother relate, with some degree of light-heartedness and humour, a story about her uncle – my Great Uncle Nicky. Nicky spent all his working life as merchant seaman. His life as a stoker was both hard and dangerous and Nicky saw wartime service both on trans-Atlantic convoys and convoys to Russia. In between these perilous voyages, he stayed with us, when he could, in Swansea. The story my mother told about Uncle Nicky's brush with heavy-handed wartime authorities became somewhat comic with the passage of time, but I remember it differently. From my point of view, as a kid, it came across as a brutal side of life in wartime, an example of how people were pressed into 'war effort' service by 'heavies' who were backed by the force of law.

The incident left a frightening impression on the seven- or eight-year-old Brian, as he witnessed the strong-arm tactics employed by the authorities in ensuring that the 'war effort' remained on track.

Brian continues,

> I can't remember exactly when the episode took place, but I remember it vividly.
>
> There was a knock on the front door, which I answered. There were two burly men. One of them asked if Nicky Barry lived here. I told them he did and called Uncle

Nicky. He was sitting at the kitchen table writing out his betting slip with a short indelible pencil. Mam joined me at the front door. The man asked again 'Does Nicky Barry live here?' Before she could answer, Nicky pushed past us facing up to the men and delivering a tirade of obscenities (totally out of character of this normally placid man), concluding with 'I'm not going on that f***ing ship!' Mam and I just stood there stunned. The men replied that they would give him five minutes to pack his things then they would take him by force if he failed to go quietly.

Uncle Nicky was a stoker in the Merchant Navy, and had been through a bad time on trans-Atlantic convoys and deserved a rest. The men were heavy press gang agents from the Merchant Navy Pool (of labour). Nicky had no option and was packed in next to no time. His suitcase wasn't very large. He was bundled into a car that rushed him away. I didn't even get my pocket money from him (which I thought was due), a twelve-sided three pence piece. I suppose his indelible pencil was safe in the waistcoat pocket of his navy blue suit. No doubt his fists were clenched, dreading the thought of shoveling coal in some hell-hole of a ship's boiler room bound for the perils of the high seas.

8

CHURCHILL COMES TO TOWN: CLOTHES ENCOUNTERS

On an overcast day in April 1941, less than two months after the centre of their town had been systematically destroyed by the Luftwaffe, the people of Swansea were paid a visit by the Prime Minister. Winston Churchill had come to inspect the damage for himself.

Until Churchill's visit (11 April 1941), there had been as many as thirty-six air raids on the town and its outlying areas, including the Three Night Blitz, which was largely responsible for the destruction of the town centre. Only three days prior to his visit, there had been an early morning raid, during which approximately 800 incendiary bombs were dropped at Mumbles Head and Limeslade. These caused gorse fires. Another bomb, a high explosive, was dropped near bungalows in a field next to Plunch Lane. This caused some damage to property but there were no casualties.

Sporting a flamboyant spotted bow tie, and with a large cigar wedged in his mouth above a firm and jutting jaw, Churchill responded to the cheering crowds with his characteristic two finger victory sign. As word got around, crowds gathered everywhere to catch a glimpse of the great man.

After meeting the dockers and praising their part in the war effort, the prime minister, accompanied by his wife, posed for photographs with civic dignitaries among the ruins of the town centre. From there, Mr Churchill walked down St Helen's Road to the Hospital Square and Swansea Hospital, gathering a crowd as he went. Clearly delighted by his visit, kids and adults ran alongside his entourage, cheering as he raised his hat high on his walking stick, waving it in acknowledgement of this happy band of followers.

STRIKING FASHION

Churchill, accompanied by his wife, visited the stricken town on 11 April 1941. While the Prime Minister was dressed both for the weather and the occasion, it seemed, to some, that Mrs Churchill's choice of outfit was hardly befitting the nature of the occasion into which she was expected to blend as a dutiful wife.

In sharp contrast to the sombre 'winter' attire of her husband (whose top hat lent a slightly archaic touch to the proceedings), and the garb of civic dignitaries and their wives, Mrs Churchill wore a 'striking' outfit. So striking that in the austerity of the times, and against the backdrop of a devastated provincial town, it raised eyebrows and drew comments that weren't altogether complimentary.

Topped and tailed in a turban and boots (and over a serviceable 'go-anyway' dark outfit) the Prime Minister's wife wore an extremely expensive and 'showy', light-coloured, shaggy ocelot fur coat. This was a gaudy fashion statement, the savagery of which competed with the fox fur collars (complete with the fox head) worn by other ladies in the party.

Such an outfit, in all probability, would not have turned a single head on the streets Mayfair, or have been out of place at a glitzy West End premier. However, amid the rubble of the distressed town, and in the midst of the soberly clad 'pillars of Swansea society', it took on a 'showy' cheapness that rendered her, in the eyes of some onlookers, as having the look and air of 'a bookie's wife'.

This remark, uttered by an adult and overheard by a child who witnessed the spectacle, remained in the mind of the child all through her life, becoming something of a benchmark in defining a type of woman who had the good fortune to spend extravagant sums on clothes, while lacking a sense of occasion.

However, attire apart, the majority people of Swansea were pleased that Mr and Mrs Churchill had taken the trouble to visit and reassure them that their difficult times and sacrifices were not without understanding in the highest levels of government.

Whether or not these comments on Mrs Churchill's appearance were justified can be judged from photographs taken on the day. (See photographs in *Swansea at War: A Pictorial Account 1939–45, South Wales Evening Post*, Nigel Arthur, pp.60–61)

After visiting casualties of bombing raids and with parting words of encouragement to hospital staff, he emerged into the Hospital Square to an enthusiastic reception from a crowd standing six deep. From there, he traveled the short distance to the Civic Centre, in a small, open car, waving to the crowds as he went. On leaving the Civic Centre, the Prime Minister decided that he and his party should take a look at the barrage balloon moored at the top end of Victoria Park near the Francis Street entrance. With Churchill at its head, the group then went down Francis Street and entered St Helen's Avenue. There, they encountered on a young Brian Owen who was standing alone on the corner.

BRIAN'S STORY

I think I was about seven or eight years of age. I had heard much about Winston Churchill on the wireless and from adult talk. I'd also seen him in the newsreels in the cinema. It was about midday, the weather was grey and I was standing on the corner of Francis Street and St Helen's Avenue. I was looking towards the Civic Centre when I saw a crowd, headed by Winston Churchill (escorted by police and other officials), walking towards me. There weren't many onlookers and there was nobody standing near me so I had a clear view. As Churchill went passed he looked straight at me and gave his victory sign. When I went home I told Mam. I can't remember what she said. I recall having had no special feeling about the event – he was just another person!

Churchill continued to visit blitz-stricken towns and cities throughout the war, an activity that did much to raise public morale. However, all this nearly came to an abrupt end in early 1942 when a flying incident took him perilously close to death.

While returning by flying boat from a visit to the United States on 17 January 1942, Churchill's plane came under fire and was nearly shot down – twice!

Having veered off course, the flying boat came under fire from German anti-aircraft guns over France. The navigational error corrected, the aircraft then appeared to British radar operators as an enemy bomber heading for Britain. The RAF scrambled six fighters to shoot it down, but as luck would have it they failed to locate the aircraft.

AUTHOR'S NOTE

This latter information was supplied to me without attribution. It has been included here to illustrate (along with other episodes in this book) the role that good luck played in many cases of wartime survival.

9

DELAYED ACTION:
KILLERS AND BOMBED-OUT RELATIVES

Bombing is a terrifying act of barbarism. To hear bombs whistling down and not know where they are going to land is terrifying enough, but delayed-action and UXBs (unexploded bombs) have a sinister terror all of their own. Their indeterminable detonation, and the fact that they had to be 'dealt with', often proved a lethal cocktail for bomb disposal engineers.

Swansea had its fair share of delayed-action and UXBs. Their discovery filled everyone with fear and, it should be said, a certain degree of fascination. They also caused a great deal of disruption with evacuations, road closures and traffic diversions. Although always an inconvenience, and the cause of much anxiety for bomb disposal crews and property owners, many of these bombs were successfully defused and taken away for safe detonation. They were, however, sometimes lethal. Graham Davies recollects a UXB found in premises on St Helen's Road, not far from where he lived.

St Helen's Road
Graham Davies recollects that 'the bomb came down the chimney'.

> One memory was that of an unexploded bomb in the post office on St Helen's Road. The bomb came down the chimney and ended up in the fireplace. My 'uncle', Mr J. H. Crews, owned a grocer's shop next door, and he was one of a group of wardens who went into the flat above the PO to confirm that it was a bomb! The flat was occupied by a former Mayor of Swansea and his wife, Mr and Mrs Rees. Having confirmed that it was indeed a bomb, they were told to get out, pronto. However, Mrs Rees was in poor health and they refused to leave. The bomb subsequently exploded and they were both killed.

Philips Parade
After one raid, a delayed-action bomb was found in Philips Parade by Swansea Hospital. Both Brian Owen and Graham Davies give independent graphic accounts of this bomb exploding unexpectedly.

Brian Owen recollects that 'suddenly there was an explosion'.

> It was lunchtime. I was standing outside our house in St Helen's Avenue. There was a delayed-action bomb by the hospital, in Philips Parade. Suddenly there was an explosion. I looked down the Avenue and saw mud, stones and debris rise about 200 feet in the air. A bomb disposal engineer was killed. The next day the traffic was diverted as the roads around the hospital were strewn with mud and rubbish.

Graham Davies and his three chums were closer to the same explosion.

> Our search for shrapnel took four of us to a garage roof of my friend's house in Kensington Crescent. We had just climbed onto the roof when there was a mighty bang. The bomb by the hospital had exploded. There was a plume of black smoke and the sky was full of black objects and dust. We scrambled off the roof to the safety of the garage itself, where we cowered laughing and listening to the clinks and thuds pattering on the tin roof above us. It was both exciting and scary. There was a war on and we were part of it.
>
> We rushed home to tell our parents what we had seen. A rumour was confirmed later. A bomb disposal officer had been killed in Philip's Parade. As he attempted to defuse the bomb, it had exploded.

Safe but Distressed

Everybody knew someone who had lost their home as a result of air raids. The pile of rubble, fractured beams, charred and broken bricks, that once was someone's home, was a heartbreaking sight. For the poor wretches that lost all but their lives, the war was a terrible ordeal for the remainder of 'the duration'. Adults and their kids struggled, daily to lead a normal existence, but their lives were greatly impoverished and their spirit was often all but broken.

As a very young child I was touched by an all-pervading feeling of despair that I experienced on a solitary visit to relatives that had been bombed out of their homes.

During the Blitz, my father's brother and sister were bombed out of their Swansea homes. Both families were rehoused by the authorities out of town, way up in the Swansea Valley, in the comparative safety of Ystalyfera. These were typical of families who had lost everything but survived the Blitz. Kids and adult were thankful to be alive, but the road back to recovery was long and arduous.

Although witnessing the reduction of their homes to a heap of rubble, none of these relatives were physically injured by the bombing. However, even to my young eyes, it was clear that everyone was still tense and badly shaken. Coping with their terrifying trauma and the loss of their house and home must have been difficult enough, but struggling to put together a new home in a strange place away from friends must have made life really hard, particularly for my father's sister. She had the added burden of bringing up a houseful of young kids, with her husband away serving in the Army at Tobruk.

Everybody who walked down the Prom during the war years couldn't help but see this war memorial, which was surrounded by large, square railings that were always locked. They also couldn't miss the memorial to the Swansea Jack – a hero dog who saved many from drowning. Both memorials attracted kids, and while we all knew the story of Swansea Jack, the story of the gun-carrying hero, who stood watch over his fallen comrade, always remained a mystery.

AN UNFORGETTABLE VISIT

I remember visiting Ystalyfera only once with my brother. We were taken to see our cousins by an uncle who was on leave from the Army. Living in greatly reduced circumstances these families were very distressed. I recall being very upset by what I heard and saw. I have little recollection of detail but the visit made me feel distinctly uncomfortable. I recall the depressing feeling seeing the desperate sadness that hung over everyone and everything. Kids seem to pick up on such feelings readily. I was extremely uneasy. I didn't know how to cope with it; all I wanted was to get away, back to familiar territory as quickly as possible. I remember being very frustrated at not being able to leave. My uncle had gone off somewhere and I had fallen out with my brother. Regrettably, I was responsible for a large gash on my brother's head. I'd hurled a stone at him in a fit of frustrated childish rage.

Although I feared the sirens and the German bombers very much, they paled to insignificance that evening in anticipation of what my mother and father would say about what I had done to my brother. He looked a terrible mess. His hair was matted and his white shirt was covered in blood.

Strangely, I have absolutely no recollection of my parent's reaction. Apart from my brothers condition, my enduring recollections of the day are to do with the unease I felt witnessing the distress of my relatives. That unease played heavily on my sense of security. I imagined my family being bombed out and it fueled more than the occasional nightmare.

On reflection, my day in Ystalyfera taught me a great deal. Not least, that childhood terror is often generated as much by fertile imagination as it is by actual fact.

10

HEALTH, FOOD & TRANSPORT

The following is a collection of memories, the majority of which, by request, have not been attributed. They are, however, worthy of inclusion because they are the observations of kids on matters of health, food and transport in the Second World War. Collectively, they paint a graphic picture of things largely forgotten. Some of these recollections are fascinating in their detail. The divergent views expressed on the general health of children is also a point of interest, the differences in perspectives possibly stemming from the influence of disparate social backgrounds.

WARTIME DIET AND CHILDREN'S HEALTH
David Davies recalls,

Most kids looked healthy, and many were probably healthier with a balanced wartime diet than they might otherwise have been.

Others had a different view:

Rickets were common among children – as were chest infections.

Poor diet might have been the cause of many children suffering from boils. I had my fair share. They were treated with a hot bread poultice to draw off the pus, which would leave holes in the skin.

Some boys at St David's School had shaved heads with blue spots covering what looked like sores. Someone told me it was ringworm. I don't know why, but I always thought that these were 'poor' children.

THE CLINICS
Part of my enduring memory of wartime was that of 'clinics. These I regarded as 'the enemy within'. As I recall, there were children's clinics in various parts of town, or maybe there was only one that had to move its location many times because of the

bombing. Anyway, I seemed to have visited them all before I was five and they were all houses of horror.

There was one, in a big house, on the corner of Eaton and Bryn-y-mor Crescents in the Uplands. Like many other kids, I hated of the place. I lived in dread of the day and the hour of my 'appointments' there. Vile though it was, I would have joyfully swallowed an extra ten spoonfuls of my daily dose of wartime cod liver oil to miss out on a dreaded 'appointment'.

I remember the Uplands clinic as a chilly, airy, forbidding place of shiny cold chrome instruments; kidney dishes; highly polished, thick, brown linoleum-covered floors and high gloss two-tone green walls. I hated this place with its brusque, heavily starched nurses adding to my discomfort and distrust. With one no nonsense commands they seemed to neutralize my mother's authority and assume total control. Pleading looks towards mother were to no avail. There were always children screaming – before, during and after 'treatment' – especially in the dental surgery on the top floor where the waiting room struck fear into all who entered.

POOR PUBLIC HEALTH

I was unlucky enough to catch TB from milk bought at a farm in the lanes at Murton. It affected the glands in my neck. Once a week my mother had to take me to a clinic in Cimla (outside Neath) for special 'sunray' treatment. About ten kids sat in a semi-circle around a sun lamp for about 10–15 minutes. There were always lots of kids waiting for their turn to get treatment, so the problem must have been widespread.

POOR PUBLIC TRANSPORT

Getting a bus back to Swansea from Neath was a nightmare. We'd queue for hours. There were few buses and when they did arrive priority was always given to workers. We wouldn't arrive home before teatime (much to my mother's distress) because she had to prepare a meal for my father who'd been working hard all day.

VICTORY PIE

On our trips to Cimla we had to have lunch in Neath (horrible food served by green uniformed 'volunteer' ladies wearing brimmed hats) in a large drafty hall. I remember something called 'Victory Pie' – it was terrible. The ladies got 'shirty' if you left anything on your plate. 'Don't you know there's a war on', they would bark at anyone or who disliked what they had on the menu, or who wanted a bigger portion.

That mention of Victory Pie had me recalling other things about food during the war. I had no problem with Lord Woolton's edict 'Lick the plate if you're hungry', which was much quoted and indulged when mother had cooked something that had great relish.

Restaurants & School Dinners
David Davies remembers,

> Restaurants kept going, somehow, with a very limited menu. I remember lunching at the Albert Hall (cinema restaurant) one day when a man at the next table groaned when he read the menu. 'Sausages?' he said. 'I had sausages yesterday, the day before and the day before that!' But the good old Albert Hall was great for me and a whole lot better than school dinners.

Horses For (Main) Courses
Mother did wonders with meagre wartime rations. She was a great improviser and managed to make all our meals tasty – with the exception of one memorable cheese and potato pie. Announced as 'something by way of a change', it certainly was – it tasted soapy and even the dog wouldn't eat it! We always had a good laugh whenever it was mentioned. We imagined that, somehow, in grating the cheese, a piece of yellow Sunlight soap had got into the act.

Then there was one day when she came home with the meat ration, which caused her some consternation. I recall her being annoyed that the butcher had gone to the back of the shop to get her order of beef and had wrapped it without showing her. At home, the unwrapped piece of meat on the kitchen table look like no piece of beef we'd ever seen before. It was strangely square without the slightest trace of fat. 'That's not beef', mother proclaimed. Nevertheless, it had to be cooked and eaten because there was no alternative. However, I noticed that my mother never ate any and when I raised this with my brother he said, 'That's because it was horse' – but it tasted OK!

Smoking: A Passing Cloud
Brian Owen recalls,

> Everyone, or so it seemed, smoked during the war – my father included.
>
> One evening, when he had settled down after his evening meal, he sent me out for a packet of ten Woodbine or Tennants. Cigarettes were scarce at the time. First I tried Prices, then Hammonds on King Edwards Road, but without luck. Finally, I got to Lewis's in the Avenue. All he had was 'Passing Cloud'. To me, all cigarettes were the same so I bought them and took them home. I can still hear my father's rebuke 'What do you think I am, a bloody Arab?' 'Passing Cloud' never entered the house again.
>
> It was not uncommon to see kids smoking, but not around adults.

Danger Everywhere
'Coughs and sneezes spread diseases' was an effective slogan because everyone used to cough or sneeze into a handkerchief in those days. We never went anywhere without a hanky. Buses displayed 'No Spitting' notices.

GREEN HILL GIRLS TURN YELLOW

Brian Owen tells a story about the girls from Green Hill.

During the war, the authorities considered that there were few jobs that women could not do at least as well as men. As a result women were directed to work in munition factories manufacturing bombs. Mother had some girl friends who lived in Green Hill that were directed into such jobs. Their work involved handling cordite – a smokeless explosive. As a result, of constantly handling this material, their skin became distinctly yellow. Propaganda persuaded these young women to take pride in their yellow skin since it marked them as important munitions workers doing their bit for the 'war effort'.

CONTAGIOUS INFECTIONS

Our Mam fell seriously ill. She had diphtheria and was admitted to Carn Goch Isolation Hospital. Diphtheria was so contagious that when we visited her we had to stand outside. We were only allowed to see her through a closed window. While she was in hospital, I was sent to Llanelli to stay with my grandfather and Auntie Bron for safety. I went to school there for a time. During my stay, there were several air raids – one spectacular one when an oil storage depot was hit. I remember thinking that nowhere was safe.

MENINGITIS IN ST HELEN'S GARRISON

There was an outbreak of meningitis among the soldiers stationed in the small garrison at the St Helen's Cricket Ground. One of the soldiers was a customer at a shop near Brynmill School, and was the possible source of the infection that led to the death of Mrs Stratton who ran the shop. This posed a great risk for the schoolchildren who were regular visitor to the shop.

11

THE AMERICANS

Graham Davies recollects,

Considering the influences of the war on life in general, the arrival of American servicemen in 1944 had quite an impact: Hershey's Chocolate, chewing gum ('Got any gum chum?'), American rugby at St Helen's, not to mention the effect on the young ladies of Swansea.

John Exall recalls the American army base near his home.

In spring 1944, Singleton Park was full of American soldiers. It was the main US Army base before D-Day.

LOVE AND OTHER BRUISES

The American army and air force poured into Britain in 1943 and although greeted with much goodwill, some of the population harboured a deep-seated resentment to their presence.

Well-fed, smartly dressed and better paid than their British counterparts, pleasure-seeking Yanks, with their glamorous film star auras, proved irresistible to many young women. American, Hollywood-style glamour was powerful and unwanted competition for war-weary British servicemen home on leave. Local young women, married and unmarried, were always getting 'involved' with American servicemen, and there were the inevitable explosive confrontations and pub brawls over female partners.

The potential for trouble in the vicinity the Patti Pavilion – a popular dance venue – and the Cricketer's Hotel, was ever present. On Friday and Saturday nights, groups of young women dressed up to the nines descended on these places from all over town for a good night out. The US Military Police were also there in force to keep the peace, but the mixture of young British and American servicemen, young ladies, music and booze was a powder keg.

In the earlier hours of the evening, when things were busy but under control, us kids from the Avenue would sit on the wall watching the crowds parading up and down. The pickings were rich as far as receiving chewing gum from passing US servicemen was concerned. However, as it got nearer our bedtimes, and people got more boisterous with

The Patti Pavilion in peacetime. During the war, it was a social hub for British and American servicemen, and a canteen for servicemen billeted in local homes. By day, it served the forces. By night, when circumstances permitted, it was a popular dance and entertainment venue for all. Outside, it was a magnet for kids asking the Yanks, 'Got any gum chum?'

drink, we could see the situation hotting up. We never saw any fights on the street, but some nights we were woken by men shouting and brawling in the lane behind the 'Cricketers'.

MURDER IN BRYNMILL

Around this time (though not necessarily in any way associated with what has been described above), the body of one young woman was found at the bottom of Rhyddings Park Road, in a little alleyway at the rear of houses on King Edwards Road. Her character was discussed widely among adults, and kids listened intently. Kids were fascinated by this crime and often visited the scene of the murder. The gossip played heavily on their fertile imaginations.

BULLY BEEF & A FAMOUS BOXER

The Americans arrived after the heaviest bombing raids were over. The centre of the Swansea had been reduced to a mass of rubble, but the streets had been cleared and the roads well defined – traffic flowed freely. There were two large US army bases, one at either end of the town, and there were jeeps and American servicemen everywhere. The Yanks were friendly and likeable – kids and Yanks were a great social mix .

Alfred John Whitby remembers the generosity of American soldiers.

> By the time I was eight or nine years old, the Americans had built an army base opposite Townhill, which is now the Gendros/Penlan area of the city. Us kids used to visit the army base during the day and were, very often, given tins of Bully Beef (which was the American version of our corned beef), bars of chocolate and chewing gum with names like 'Ukatan', 'Dentine' and 'Juicyfruit'. American servicemen understood that rationing was strict on us and most treats scarce but, through their contact with kids, and their natural generosity, they were able to help families.

Cyril Gronert recalled how kids hung around the same army base and ran errands for the soldiers. Apparently fish and chips were very popular with the Yanks. Cyril also recalls a famous visitor to the American troops. His friend actually shook hands with the great Joe Louis, the world boxing champion, outside a club in Morriston where he'd come to meet the US servicemen.

HALLOWED TURF AND GENEROUS YANKS

The generosity of American service men to British kids was legendary.

John Exall recalls,

> I went to Brynmill School, which was just around the corner from where I lived. Our teacher Mr W. G. Williams was a rugby enthusiast, and one day he took us on a school

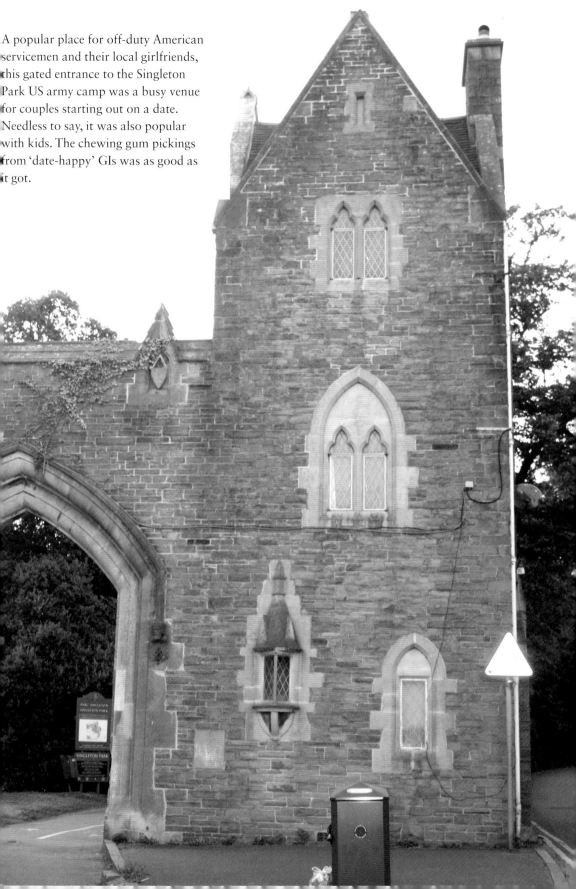

A popular place for off-duty American servicemen and their local girlfriends, this gated entrance to the Singleton Park US army camp was a busy venue for couples starting out on a date. Needless to say, it was also popular with kids. The chewing gum pickings from 'date-happy' GIs was as good as it got.

trip to St Helen's Rugby Ground. The highlight of the visit was to stand near the pitch at the Mumbles End to see the spot where Denny Hunt had scored the winning try for the All Whites against New Zealand.

I was standing at the back and so edged forward onto the pitch to see the hallowed piece of turf. Mr Williams pointed at me and bellowed: 'Don't you ever put a foot on that rugby ground unless you are playing.'

Not long after that incident, the American army touring rugby team, 'The Screaming Eagles', played a selected team from the Army bases in Swansea. It was probably the biggest attendance ever seen at St Helen's.

In the first ten minutes, after a crash tackle, one of the players broke his leg and had to be carried off. From the Mumbles End, an old MASH-type ambulance appeared, and the stricken player was placed inside. Surprisingly, the ambulance did a lap of honour around the ground before leaving and I watched it churn up the wet ground exactly on the hallowed piece of turf in the corner. As a twelve-year-old, I wondered what Mr W. G. Williams would say.

I was a programme seller at the ground on that day. Two pence a copy in old pennies. As usual, the American soldiers were very generous, and on a number of occasions I was given a half-crown or 2s piece and told to keep the change. It was a bumper day. I earned over £8 in tips, which was an enormous sum. It was over three times the weekly £2 3s 6d my Mum received from the Forces Allowance for the upkeep of herself and three children. I went home very pleased, with sagging pockets.

A WELCOME GIFT
John Exall remembers a thoughtful priest and his generous gift.

The name of the Roman Catholic padre, with the troops, was Father Schultz and he struck up a friendship with Father O'Keefe of my church, St Benedict's.

As a result of this friendship, many young American soldiers used to attend evening service in the church, and then stay on afterwards to join us in the youth club. I got to know quite a few. Father Schultz saw to it that we weren't short of equipment. In typical generous American style, he arranged for a load of sports equipment to be delivered to the club hall. Baseball bats, balls, catching gloves, pads and boxing gloves were piled in the centre of the hall. It sounds ungrateful, but we weren't able to use them. The American rugby balls did get some use, however – we used to throw them to each other in the hall.

12

DESTINATION NORMANDY

The buzz of life that descended on the town with the arrival of the Americans was to disappear as fast as it had arrived. The day of their departure from Swansea was a well-kept secret, yet the spectacle of their embarkation for Normandy and the D-Day landings was on an epic scale. Although their departure was much anticipated as the war progressed, it came as a 'bolt from the blue' to all, and with much personal heartache for some.

By and large, the 'Yanks' were seen as friendly, fun-loving and generous. They brought a vitality and a certain amount of glamour to the social life to the town. For local kids, they were a welcome injection into the prevailing culture; new sayings and the gum-chewing habit quickly took hold. For us kids, their departure was to be the end of an era. For so many families in the USA, it was the curtain-raiser on devastating tragedy. Many of these young men and their 'folks back home' were about to pay the ultimate price for victory and freedom for us all.

BOUND FOR A FOREIGN FIELD

There was something of a pre-echo of the coming tragedy in what a young Brynmill boy, **John Exall**, witnessed at an evening church service in St Benedict's in Sketty. The essence of that tragedy still lingers in the way he tells it.

John recollects the poignance of an American sergeant's words.

> I was twelve years of age at the time, but I was aware that these young soldiers would shortly be going overseas to fight for the Allies, and many would not return. At the evening service, an American sergeant was taking the collection and he came up to a GI who seemed to be having difficulty in choosing the right coin. I remember the words of the sergeant: 'Put it all in son. You ain't going to need that where you're going.'

Graham Davies also recollects a very moving interlude.

> I have vague memories of a very moving Easter concert/service given in the Brangwyn Hall for the troops in 1944 before D-Day. I didn't attend but I remember my mother being moved to tears. Dame Eva Turner sang the *Easter Hymn*.

WE'LL MEET AGAIN

Short though it was, the duration of the American 'occupation' of Swansea had forged many strong bonds between the townspeople and the US servicemen. Now, all that was at an end. Their arrival boosted morale, their departure left a definite gap.

The songs 'Wish Me Luck As You Wave Me Goodbye' and 'We'll Meet Again' caught the spirit of it all, but behind the bouncy 'go-get-'em' and 'come home safe' sentiment, there was punishing heartbreak and real tragedy ahead, along with a deep-seated sense of loss in its wake – no less for Swansea kids. Yanks and kids got on famously. When asked 'got any gum chum?', the Yanks invariably responded generously. Now, with their embarkation, there was to be one final chorus of the much-heard phrase, along the convoy of departing Americans, then it would be gone forever. While much could be written about the departure of the Americans, for the beaches of Normandy and how it affected the lives of the people of Swansea, the focus on just a few recollections of kids (for whom the day was memorable both for

'The Armada in the Bay'. The day the troops left Swansea bound for D-Day landings in Normandy, recorded in this sketch by Brian Owen. It is recounted by him, and other Brynmill boys, as a spectacle of epic proportions.

its spectacle and for the emotions it evoked) will provide a flavour of the event as seen through the eyes of children.

THE ARMADA IN THE BAY

It first dawned on ten-year-old Brian Owen, that there was something big afoot when he arrived at the high ground at the top of the Mayals. Brian was cycling back home to Brynmill from the family bungalow in Miles Field in Murton, when he saw an awesome sight.

Brian Owen recalls,

> I was coming home from the bungalow, over Fairwood Common and passed Nazareth House on my bike. I was with someone, but can't remember who. As Swansea Bay came into sight, just before reaching the top of the Mayals, I couldn't believe my eyes – the bay was packed with hundreds of ships.

From every vantage point, kids spent hours looking at the huge armada gathered in the bay, wondering where they came from, what they were doing there, where they were going. Some tried counting them while most just stood and marveled at the spectacle.

John Exall recalls the sight from Brynmill:

> Out at sea there was a mass of ships obscuring the horizon.

KIDS AND CONVOYS

The sound of high volume traffic went out like a clarion call. Kids from everywhere swarmed to the roads leading to the docks. A great convoy was heading for embarkation. The invasion of mainland Europe was on. The Yanks were leaving. Some kids recall the spectacle and their emotions.

John Exall recalls,

> I lived in Langland Terrace, Brynmill with my mum, brother and sister. Dad was away in the Forces. One morning after breakfast I could hear a strange thrumming, throbbing sound. It was coming from the Mumbles Road, which was just around the corner from where we lived. I went down to the front to see what was happening.
>
> I saw the biggest traffic jam ever seen on the Mumbles Road. A huge convoy of US army lorries and other military vehicles was moving slowly on the Mumbles Road towards the town centre and on to the docks. Apparently, the queue stretched for miles from the docks back past the entrance to Singleton Park. The thrumming noise of the vehicles was almost overpowering. It was Embarkation Day. The young soldiers I had met in church were on their way to France.

Brian Owen recalls,

> We didn't know it at the time, but the Americans, camped at Singleton, were preparing for the invasion of Normandy. Rows of tank carriers and lorries lined the Mumbles Road. The GIs were cleaning rifles and sorting out their equipment. A friend and I begged for candy and chewing gum. We called out to the soldiers 'Any gum chum?'
>
> The LMS railway, which ran from Victoria Station (now the site of the leisure centre) around the Bay until it turned off up into Clyne Valley at Blackpill, was very busy. From the 'Brown Bridge', which crossed the railway line at Swansea Bay station (situated opposite the cricket field), we watched trains bringing tanks and big guns to the docks.

A Mystery

I remember on the day that the Americans were leaving, while we were playing in the street, at the cricket field end of St Helen's Avenue, we heard the unusual sound of heavy traffic on the Mumbles Road. When we got there, there was this huge convoy of lorries and armoured vehicles. The Yanks were leaving!

Kids from everywhere descended on the convoy as it moved slowly towards the docks. The Yanks were, as ever, generous. They were throwing kids bars of chocolate and chewing gum from their passing vehicles. I was standing next to a group of Brynmill kids, who had gathered at the end of the Rec (the recreation ground) next to the cricket field. The convoy had come to a halt. Some bigger boys were telling their friends about seeing, some days earlier, Yankee soldiers, burying sacks in Singleton Park and the soldiers had told them to go away. These kids were speculating about what the Yanks had buried in those sacks. This both interested and disturbed me, for while guns and some sort of treasure were mentioned, they also said that the soldiers had to kill their dogs because nobody wanted them and they couldn't take them with them.

Had it not been for the mention of the fate of the dogs, in all probability what I had heard would have gone in one ear and out the other, but the idea of killing dogs alarmed and distressed me. I remember trying to tell my brother what I'd heard, but by this time the convoy was on the move again, everyone's interest had swung back to the soldiers throwing candy and chewing gum to the kids from the moving convoy.

I loved dogs and the dog story worried me greatly. I told my mother. She reassured me that nobody would kill healthy dogs. So exactly what the soldiers had buried in Singleton Park remained a mystery.

All in all, it was a day of mixed emotions. The bit about the dogs; the squabbles among kids over the begged goodies; the confused feeling of embarrassment when begging sometimes went unrewarded (for whatever reason). Greed, childish though it all was, revealed itself as a powerful disruptive force. I learned much that day and still recall the event with mixed emotions and feelings of deep-seated embarrassment.

My one regret was that I never saw the armada in the bay. We couldn't cross the busy road to the beach, and I had strict instructions to stay close to my brother because I was too young to go off anywhere by myself.

A MEMENTO
John Exall recalls,

After the war, Father Schultz (the US army padre) sent Father O'Keefe a chalice to be placed in St Benedict's church. It was the one he had used on the Normandy beaches.

13

'ITS OVER!':
BUT WHAT DID THIS MEAN TO KIDS?

There is very little recorded information on how children responded to the news that the war was over. We know that adults greeted the official announcement with great jubilation. There was a spontaneous eruption of joy and celebration everywhere, and kids joined in, but what did the end of the war mean to those children who knew nothing other than times of war? Maybe kids found it too hard to comprehend. Were concepts like the 'end of hostilities' and the 'restoration of the peace' just too abstruse to make an impact on young minds conditioned to war? Maybe children were simply bewildered by the reactions of adults – reactions so uncharacteristically intense that kids became fascinated onlookers, their own feelings and reactions paling to insignificance. Perhaps they felt a sense of regret and disappointment that a great adventure was about to end, while apprehensive as to what would fill the void. Maybe they were caught up in an already burgeoning freedom and saw the announcement of the end of the war as merely an inevitable formality – an official pronouncement to set the seal on things. Possibly their feelings about the declaration of the peace was a mixture of all these things.

SILENT KIDS
Whatever the reason, the record regarding kids' reactions to the end of the war, is, to all intents and purposes, non-existent. In one of only two recollections offered here, **Graham Davies** summed it up succinctly: 'We were too young to appreciate it fully.'

> May 1945. End of the war. My friend Stuart and I were waiting at the stage door of the Swansea Empire Theatre collecting autographs. Ella Retford, a famous music hall artiste of her day, signed our books and asked us to wait. She returned within a few minutes with signed photographs of herself, and then to our surprise hugged each of us in turn. We were both bemused and embarrassed until she gushed, 'The war is over!' – a marvellous example of spontaneous joy. We were too young to appreciate it fully.

VE Day St Helen's Avenue. Kids, mums and a family dog tucked into a party like no other. Note the absence of men, most of whom were away at war. That night, this stretch or road became an open-air dance floor festooned with fairy lights and bunting, while music serenaded servicemen and women, and a host of passers by, under a canopy of stars. This was one special night with no early bedtime for kids.

The threat of German bombs was long since over, and life was now less fractured by emergency. As much as they were able, people were picking up the pieces, getting on with their lives and anticipating the safe return of their loved ones. Gas masks gathered dust on shelves and shrapnel continued to be swapped, but gone were the mornings of souvenir hunting and discovery. The smell and dust of war was clearing, the nights of terror were fading into memory, but the war that had so completely dominated young lives now denied them vision of the future. So profound was the effect of war on children's lives that some had difficulty contemplating any alternative. This is illustrated by the following childhood memory.

As a seven-year-old, I recall thinking 'there won't be any news because there's no war to report.' It seemed there were only two things we heard on the news in those days – news about how the war was going and announcements about measures to be implemented in terms of the 'war effort'. So, in my bewilderment, never having been exposed to anything other than wartime news, it was beyond me as to what they would have to say in peacetime.

This scarcity of recollections underscores the extent to which we lack information about children's reactions to an occasion of some great moment in the twentieth century.

That the war was over was a joy that showed on the relaxed faces of the VE Day party mums, but for kids the peace was a dramatic change that was hard to come to grips. 'What now?' was the question behind all those serious young faces.

14

VE DAY, 1945

Germany surrendered on 7 May 1945 and victory in Europe was declared the next day. Although the war with Japan was not yet over, to all intents and purposes, for the people of Great Britain, 8 May 1945 (VE Day) was the first day of the hard-won peace, and they went wild with excitement.

The streets of Swansea were awash with red, white and blue paint. Curb and paving stones, lamp posts and dustbins – everything that could take a coat of paint was daubed with the national colours. Union Jacks appeared everywhere, painted on pavements and in the middle of roads. Large flags were draped across many front-room windows, while smaller versions fluttered from sticks poked through upstairs windows. Colourful bunting, attached from drainpipe to drainpipe, criss-crossed streets at roof level, and everywhere was made ready for a great day of celebration.

BONFIRES AND STREET PARTIES

Around mid-morning, amid all this frenzied activity, a great buzz went around kids all over town that there were to be large bonfires that evening, and we all set about collecting whatever we could. Great hoards of junk appeared from everywhere. This was carted off to the site of the fire where it was stacked in a huge heap ready for the 'big burn' that evening.

Inspection of rivals' bonfires was routinely undertaken – everyone was determined that their bonfire was going to be the biggest and best. More rubbish was gathered and bonfires were stacked so high that they became unstable and had to be rebuilt. By early afternoon, most bonfires were ready, and a guard was mounted to ward off the real threat of plunder or premature torching by rival 'gangs'.

Then came the next big surprise – a party was to be laid on for us kids in the middle of the road. These parties became the trademark of VE Day everywhere.

Our party in St Helen's Avenue seemed typical of street parties everywhere. Kids seated, mothers in attendance and dogs under the huge long table being fed tasty morsels of the party fare.

Nobody cared what time kids went to bed that evening. The bonfires were spectacular. Loudspeakers were rigged up in streets all over town and pumped out much-loved Glenn Miller music into the warm night. Streets everywhere became dance

The author (in sailor suit) with street friends on VE Day 1945.

halls and everyone danced, sang, hugged, kissed and drank the night away. Pubs were drunk dry and, by night's end, total strangers had become firm friends.

AN IMPROMPTU CONCERT

There was much that was memorable for everyone on VE Day. **Graham Davies** recalls some moments from his day.

Great celebrations were held on the Civic Centre greens, where thousands of revelers gathered to celebrate the good news. Issy Bonn, top of the bill in the Swansea Empire that week, gave an impromptu concert from the steps of the main entrance to the Civic Centre. One of his songs was 'My Russian Rose'. On the same night, a sailor managed to gain access to the clock tower and from a precarious position waved to the massed crowds below.

'Typical VE Day Street Party', an observant sketch from memory by Brian Owen. Note the low walls in front of some of the houses. Once topped by ornate iron railings, one day, without notice, these were unceremoniously removed by gangs of workmen and carried away for the war effort.

JOE'S ICE CREAM PARLOUR

As part of the celebration of VE Day, ice-cream was free in Joe's Ice Cream Parlour. A large queue formed and my friends, Bryn and Cliffy Jones (who later played for Spurs and Wales), were put in charge of the queue. Some 'greedies', licking their free ices, rejoined the queue for a second time.

It was a very warm and kind gesture on Joe Cascarini's part, when you remember that the windows of his shop were smashed when Italy entered the war on Germany's side in 1940.

A final word from Graham, about the conclusion to his war, sums it up for many of us.

VE Day celebrations. I only have vague memories of street parties where there was dancing in the streets. They were very happy times and there was a marvellous generosity of spirit between people everywhere – we had been through something awful together and now was the time for letting go.

EPILOGUE

Apart from those kids who lost homes and loved ones, and whose lives were permanently scarred by the misfortunes of war, with the end of hostilities most Swansea kids had little reason to look back on their wartime distress. Shrapnel collections eventually went out with the rubbish and, apart from lingering nightmares, nights of uninterrupted sleep became a soothing balm to strained and tattered young nerves. Even though the population was still bearing the brunt of rationing and other wartime privations, children's post-war lives were too full, and kids were too preoccupied with their new, peaceful world to dwell on the immediate past. Their wartime recollections were simply put aside.

The physical scars of war were still there. The bombed sites, though now cleared and leveled, presented a gaping void in the centre of the town. Children locked away their mental scars as much as they were able. Post-war life promised great prospect and wartime kids thrived on prospect.

There was a new sense of freedom everywhere and our small worlds expanded with this newfound freedom. Travel restrictions were lifted and places became more accessible. Now you could go wherever you pleased. Gone were the days when posters confronted you with 'Is your journey really necessary?' The residents of St Helen's Avenue 'clubbed together' and hired a yellow Swan bus to take us on a day's picnic to a mystery destination on Gower. The bus, packed with parents, kids and bags filled with bottles of pop and soggy tomato sandwiches took us to Crawley Woods, where its stream, dunes, beach and woods presented us with a magical adventure playground on that glorious summer's day.

The excitement of the Odeon cinema in Sketty every Saturday morning charged our imaginations. Occasional visits to Joe's Ice Cream Parlour provided such treats as knickerbocker glories, while the delights of Dan Morgan's toy shop on the corner of Dillwyn Street and St Helen's Road, together with toy stalls in the market, changed our focus, dispelling thoughts of the terrifying darkness of wartime nights with all their dangers.

Momentarily, kids were all dazzled by the offerings of peacetime. The blaze of lights that festooned Studt's first post-war fair on the Rec at Brynmill caught and heightened the excitement of the peace. For me, rides on Henry Studt's dazzling carousel, to the accompaniment of the latest hit 'Shine on Harvest Moon', not only gave pleasure to the moment, but filled my head full of prospect.

In this heady post-war atmosphere, there was no thought about what perils peacetime might hold. For many, however, their newfound peace was shrouded in the numbness of loss of many kinds. Some kids, whose fathers were wounded, or were prisoners of war, found their Dads were now 'somehow different'. Physically and mentally broken, some war veterans had a difficult time readjusting. Family life often suffered.

For a brief moment, the Second World War came back to haunt us. I recall somehow knowing, though having no idea of time zones, that at a given time, on a particular day in August 1945, an atomic bomb was to be dropped on a city in Japan. I remember it was a sunny day with big, white cumulus clouds in the direction of Kilvey Hill. At the appointed time, a group of us kids in St Helen's Avenue just stood and watched the sky. We had heard that the sky might catch fire and that it would be the end of the world. We held our breath. Thankfully it wasn't, but for us kids it seemed a distinct possibility. We had come to expect such horrors from war. Conditioned by horrendous destruction, we had been reduced to fascinated spectators.

Nobody escaped the horrors of war; we had all endured them for years. Our emotions had been wrung out and our nerves frayed, but now there was respite – but not for everyone. For some poor souls, the horrors seemed never-ending and the agony just went on and on.

MRS PERRY RECEIVED HER LONG-DREADED TELEGRAM

Killed at Arnhem, she had lost a son. Dorothy had lost a brother and peacetime was no easy place for Cyril Perry's grieving widow and their three young children, who so desperately yearned to have their Dad back home with them to share the peace.